PARTNERS IN PRODUCTION

A New Role for Management and Labor

From 48 years of strike-free experience a pioneer of management gives an answer to the greatest question of our time: Can free enterprise survive the economic challenge of Communism?

Every man who knows how to read has it in his power to magnify himself, to multiply the ways in which he exists, to make his life full, significant and interesting.

—ALDOUS HUXLEY

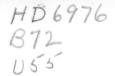

PARTNERS IN PRODUCTION

A New Role for Management and Labor

by
HENRY LIGHTFOOT NUNN

Englewood Cliffs, N.J.
PRENTICE HALL, INC.

In sincere appreciation, this book is dedicated to the officers, counselors, and business agents of the INDUSTRIAL UNION OF MASTER CRAFTSMEN with whom I worked in harmony and mutual trust for thirty-five years.

Library of Congress
Catalog Card Number: 61–12042

PRINTED IN THE UNITED STATES OF AMERICA
65146—MO

PREFACE

> Labor is prior to and independent of capital. Capital is only the fruit of labor, and could never have existed if labor had not first existed. Labor is the superior of capital and deserves much the higher consideration.

These words of President Abraham Lincoln, from his first annual message to Congress on December 3, 1861, were qualified as follows:

> Capital (also) has its rights, which are as worthy of protection as any other rights.

Who can doubt that if Lincoln were living today, he still would be concerned with the inequality of opportunity for economic gain by those who have only their hands and minds to aid them as compared with those who have by inheritance, exceptional ability and sacrifice, or some good fortune succeeded in accumulating and enjoying the fruits of labor.

If there is disagreement on this observation, there can be none on the proposition that conflict between those who supply the tools of industry and those who use them is wasteful, and that the greatest gains for both capital and labor as well as the consuming public can best be attained through cooperation.

In the mistaken belief that capital takes all the risk, and that its rights are prior to those of labor, capital has for too long struggled to achieve this cooperation through the device of "welfare" plans sometimes based on a spirit of paternalism or altruism, sometimes as a method of preventing labor organization and collective action, and usually with the basic misconception that labor is a commodity to be manipulated primarily for the greater benefit of capital interests.

Leaders of organized labor, too, have often allowed themselves to be trapped by this same false conception. On occasion, they have asserted that labor is a commodity and that as the sellers they have a right to set the price. They have also staunchly maintained that labor does not belong on the same side of the table as management and shares no common interest with management.

In this book, I endeavor to point out how an industrial organization, leaving the path of custom, discovered that the practical application of the principles of democracy and equality eradicated this false premise from the thinking of capital and labor leadership; that principles of democracy, rather than benevolence and paternalism on the part of management, proved much more potent in developing cooperation and demonstrated a more profitable and satisfying relationship to all interests alike—capital, management and labor.

Part I of the book tells the story of an economic relationship born in July 1935 out of the experience gained during one of the most disastrous periods in American industrial history—the years following the great financial debacle of October 1929.

Chapter 1 contains a description of *The Nunn-Bush Share-Production Plan,* which developed from this experience. The three succeeding chapters tell the story of the plan's conception, the history of its first exciting years after its initial acceptance by the workers, and its later evolution.

In Part II, attention is called to the social and psychological phases of labor relationships. Without a sound understanding of these factors, no entirely successful economic relationship can be developed. The more I reflect upon my own years of industrial experience, the more I become convinced that it is to the Nunn-Bush management's recognition of these social and psychological factors that the success of their economic relationship with labor must be attributed. Without this understanding, the Share-Production plan would never have been born; without constant concern for these factors, it could never have survived and attained success. To me, the ideas in Part II are the most important contribution of this book.

The first chapter of Part II relates the Nunn-Bush management's early efforts to find a better way in these all-important social and psychological phases of labor relations and the evolution of a better understanding which resulted. In it I describe the gradual changes in management's thinking that ultimately led them to relinquish the power to make decisions unilaterally and the highly satisfactory results of that policy for both capital and labor. Subsequent chapters point out some of the causes of the working man's discontent and some of the reasons why management has traditionally been unable to secure the cooperation of labor that it so diligently seeks, as well as additional suggestions for the better future relationships to which better mutual understanding will logically lead.

The reader should keep in mind, however, that in pursuit of a better way, the management was always concerned, first and foremost, with the capital interests of the business. We considered ourselves motivated solely by self-interest. We made no claim to moral excellence. Everything done was first subjected to this test: Will it be profitable for management and the capital interests?

Even so, it was rewarding to realize that by finding a way to give workers more regular and more uniform pay, based on a fair share of values added to raw materials, and by emphasizing annual income rather than wage rates, we had given the worker greater security and self-respect and had built a *common* enterprise, one that benefited the workers as much as it did management and stockholders. We were truly partners in production.

I hope that students in our academic institutions, and men and women in the field of industrial management and labor leadership, will read this story of a search along new and hitherto unexplored paths. It is especially for men and women whose minds are not closed to principles of industrial democracy that this book has been written.

For obvious reason fictitious names have been used in a few of the anecdotes I have related, but in the majority of instances the names are real and in every instance the story is true.

Some readers may have little or no interest in the first part of the book. I suggest that they read the second part first.

I should point out that I have no official connection with the Nunn-Bush Shoe Company and have not had since November 1, 1950. The views expressed are entirely my own.

In conclusion I wish to express my thanks to my wife, Josephine, for her assistance and patience; to Helen Teague, Louise Drew and Doris Roehm for faithful secretarial work; to Frances Torbert, Hubert A. Somervell, William Menton, Claude Dudley, Edgar A. Jones, Jr., Quentin Ogren, Currin V. Shields, Clinton S. Golden and Allen W. Rucker for friendly suggestions.

I am particularly indebted to David D. Malcolm, Louis C. Ritter and Harry Newman, Jr., for editorial assistance that was invaluable. Harry Newman, in particular, not only inspired me to start the project but was my constant advisor every step of the way.

INTRODUCTION

Many of the social and political ideas which have most profoundly influenced the mind of man and consequently altered the course of history seem so obvious, so inevitable in retrospect, that it is surprising to us now that they ever could have encountered apathy or opposition. It is even more remarkable how consistently these reforms have crystallized in the convictions and efforts of one man, who did not accept conditions as they were, but looked at them with a fresh and critical eye.

Although it is unusual for these innovators to be able to test their ideas in practice, Henry L. Nunn is such a man. He saw the basic flaws in the management-labor relationship and produced a workable solution which is applicable wherever one man hires another to do work.

His pioneering achievements over a half century stemmed from his recognition of two simple but basic human principles, which were—and still are to a great extent—violated in management-labor relations.

First, he found that man inherently resents and, whenever possible, rebels against arbitrary authority.

Secondly, he learned at first hand the pernicious, undermining effects of job insecurity and arbitrary power on man's self-respect and dignity.

These two discoveries were not dramatic revelations. They evolved from his early unquestioning acceptance of what he found in shoe factories as the ordained, immutable facts of industrial life. Management took the economic risk. Labor was a commodity to be bought, used and discarded. Management's word was law, unless of course you chose to try to find work elsewhere.

His first target was arbitrary authority. In 1919 by inserting a provision in the Nunn-Bush Union contract guaranteeing the right of arbitration in any case of disagreement between management and labor on *any* issue, he abolished arbitrary authority. This seemingly simple but revolutionary concept is Henry Nunn's greatest single contribution to management.

The renunciation of its so-called prerogatives of ultimate and arbitrary authority provided management with a sure means of creating a harmonious working atmosphere, of substituting a cooperative partnership for the conventional power relationship with its suppressed resentment and grudging compliance. By exchanging its traditional "rights" for mutual rights with labor, management earned a new right—the right to have its decisions wholeheartedly implemented by the workers.

Henry Nunn not only recognized but proved in 48 years of strike-free and arbitration-free practice how such a policy could revolutionize the attitudes of both sides by raising one of the partners, labor, to equal psychological status with the other. "A man can stand to be poor," Mr. Nunn is fond of saying, "but he can't stand to be nothing."

His second objective was job security for the worker. To achieve it, he devised the 52-Paychecks-a-Year Plan, later called Share-Production, in which income is tied to the value added by labor to the raw material of the manufactured product. Although this plan can be adapted to benefit workers in a wide range of industries, Mr. Nunn believes that this contribution to the labor movement will be measured by the success of his efforts to change labor's concern from wage "rates" to "wages."

"It's the amount of money a man takes home in a year that counts," he often points out. "Whether he is earning $1.00 or $3.00 an hour doesn't make much difference if he is employed only a few months of the year and never knows when he is going to be laid off." He thinks much of the union's efforts has been wasted in pursuing this chimera of wage "rates" while neglecting the basic issues of job security and dependable annual income.

Although the book traces the evolution of Mr. Nunn's philosophy and describes in detail the methods he employed to gain acceptance for his ideas among the workers, it leaves unanswered

one vital question. How much of the success of the program depended on his presence and personality?

Henry Nunn is a non-conformist, an innovator, not a reforming
eccentric. At the age of 83 he drives a red sports car. He prefers
the company of a working man to the formalities of society. He
used to enjoy bowling with the workers, eating with them, attend-
ing company dances and picnics. He dislikes artifice in any form
and considers the accumulation and display of wealth a waste
of energy.

Last year at Christmas (he left Nunn-Bush in 1950) he received 144 letters and cards from the workers and almost as many
on his birthday. They relate incidents in factory life, reminisce
about earlier days ("you were always like a father to me") or
describe their retirement. The following excerpt is typical:

> It was a pleasure to work for Nunn-Bush those 32 years
> and at this time want to thank you again for all you done
> for the workers. Starting up all the different plans includ-
> ing the 52 pay check plan which gained attention all over
> the United States, also the profit sharing and retirement
> plan which gives the worker some protection and security
> after retirement. I must not forget the favor and good work
> you done for the workers as Chief World Series announcer
> at the factory. We were always glad to see you do us that
> favor, but from now on I might be able to see the world
> series in my own home. I already have a reserved seat right
> behind the catcher.

From these letters one gets a clear picture of H.L.'s (that is the
way they address him) relationship with the workers. They obviously feel they can confide in him. They respect him for his
objective attitude and fairness. They like him as a friend. There
is no adulation, no deference, just simple and direct communication from one friend to another.

Once when he read a review of his first book, *The Whole Man
Goes to Work*, praising him as a "good" man for his worthy
projects, H.L. snorted, "Why heck, I'm not a *good* man. I may be
fair and I may be a good businessman, but I'm not *good*." Perhaps
we can see him in sharpest perspective through the eyes of one
of his closest associates who wrote to him:

You are absolutely correct when you say that if you had
had an academic education, you might not have had the
common touch. To me, you see, your personal and remarkable individual value lies in precisely the fact that you went
into a living situation *without* a preconceived academic
framework of economic theory, where your heart and head
played *equal* parts in developing new concepts, new relationships, new values—in an area of modern life where
they are desperately needed. Nothing new comes out of
the intellect by itself—in spite of our age's having substi-
tuted the intellect for God.

It has been more than ten years since Mr. Nunn's departure
from the company. The Share-Production Plan and Contract are
still in full effect. Changes continue to be made as required by
new circumstances, but the principles are intact. The management, convinced of the practical benefits of the program, have
lent it their support. Mr. Nunn believes, and the evidence sup-
ports his view, that once the proper climate of opinion has been
created and the program has been tried and proved, it will continue to flourish.

The principles of the Nunn-Bush Plan are by no means limited
to one industry. They apply to any business involving workers
and managers. The problem is to change attitudes, substitute influence for power, qualified security for insecurity, thus making a
partnership instead of an armed camp out of industry.

One of the elder statesmen of industrial relations, Clinton S.
Golden, summed it up in a letter to Mr. Nunn as follows:

As a next step I would like to see a move in the direction
you have so successfully taken. But here we encounter all
sorts of resistance. On the management side an almost ir-
rational defense of management prerogatives as if they
were divinely ordained. On the union side a deeply ingrained folklore that there is no mutuality of interest; that
management tolerates the union, but does not accept it as a
legitimate institution and therefore seeks an opportunity
to destroy it or at least render it ineffectual.

In this atmosphere new vested interests in potentially
continuing the conflict emerge. These are the lawyers on

both sides, the professional arbitrators and numerous va-
rieties of *experts* employed by either or both parties.
Added also is the problem of *bigness* in both unions and
corporate enterprises and the impersonality of relationships that result therefrom.

I am convinced that these problems can be solved, but
I fear that the solutions are more likely to arise out of desperation than by processes of persuasion and education.
Certainly these innovators like yourself have made and
are making contributions to a better way, the value of
which will some day be recognized.

We are living in an age of organization. I think unions
have an important role. But it must be a changing one.
Neither they nor management nor corporate organizations
can continue to relive the past and *back* into the future.
In some way a sense of common purpose must be encouraged to grow and expand. Some way must be found that
will enable two separate and distinct sovereign organizations—the union of the workers and that of the enterprise—to live and work together cooperatively and cre-
atively. You have demonstrated that this is possible.

HARRY NEWMAN JR.
B.A., I.A. (Harvard) M. Litt. (Cantab.)

Long Beach, California

BIOGRAPHICAL SKETCH

Henry L. Nunn

1878
Born in Bonham, Texas. Son of John Milton and Sallie Heiston Nunn. Father was a successful merchant until forced into bankruptcy during the financial panic of 1873. Father later became a travelling salesman for a men's clothing manufacturer.

1886–
1894
Attended various private and public elementary schools in Bonham and St. Louis, Mo. up to and including seventh grade. Then completed his formal education with a bookkeeping course at Jones Commercial College in St. Louis, Mo.

1894–
1897
Returning to Bonham, established a small weekly newspaper which was liquidated after a few months.

1898
Enlisted and appointed First Sergeant in Company "M" First Texas Volunteers for service in Spanish-American war.

1898
After five months' service, received honorable discharge at end of war.

1899
With Cliff A. Jones established the Nunn & Jones Company, men's-wear retail store at Bonham, Texas.

1899
Married Josephine Ewing of Bonham. Six children, five surviving.

1903
Dissatisfied with restricted opportunities of a small town, moved to St. Louis, Mo. and, through newspaper ad secured position as office manager in large shoe factory owned by Roberts, Johnson & Rand Shoe Co.

1904
Promoted to general assistant supervisor in factory.

1905
Promoted to foreman of Fitting Department and later in the year to superintendent of factory.

1907   Organized and became superintendent of the Cape Girar-
        deau, Mo. factory, Roberts, Johnson & Rand Shoe Co.

1908   Contracted tuberculosis and leaving his family in Bonham,
        Texas, spent five months in Agnes Memorial Sanatarium,
        Mont Clair, Colorado.

1908   After spending a few months with family in Bonham, Texas,
        drove a team of horses through various parts of western
        Texas finally settling in San Antonio.

1909   Brought family to San Antonio, purchased automobile and
        drove it in livery for five months.

1909   Accepted an offer of Roberts, Johnson & Rand Shoe Co. to
        cover a territory in western Texas in the capacity of travel-
        ling salesman.

1910   Returned to St. Louis and general factory service.

1910   After five months of limited service, became impatient with
        inactivity and accepted position as superintendent of fac-
        tory Harsh & Edmonds Shoe Co., Milwaukee, Wisconsin.

1912   Organized the Nunn & Bush Shoe Co. Name later changed
        to Nunn, Bush & Weldon Shoe Co. and later still to the
        Nunn-Bush Shoe Co.

1915   Initiated the policy of relinquishing managerial preroga-
        tives of arbitrary unilateral action in relations with com-
        pany employees.

1918   Appointed Executive Assistant to Chief of Shoe Division,
        U.S. Army Quartermaster Department in Washington, D.C.

1918   Served in France on a special mission for the Quarter-
        master General.

1918   Returned to factory at end of war.

1919   Completed transition of factory from open shop with ortho-
        dox management-labor relations to a closed Association
        shop with all employees required to be members of worker
        organization.

1919   The company purchased the Menzies Shoe Company of
        Detroit, Michigan, manufacturers of men's and boy's heavy
        footwear, and, combining it with similar footwear made in
        their Milwaukee factory, established it in a new factory

in Fond du Lac, Wisconsin as a separate division of the company.

1920–
1921   Overexpansion of business, large inventories with collapse of prices caused heavy losses and financial crisis.

1921   Weldon retired from company. Nunn was given charge of finances as well as manufacturing.

1921   Decision made to concentrate and specialize on high-grade men's shoes.

1921   Sold Menzies division of the company as part of plan to liquidate assets unnecessary in the building of a men's fine-shoe manufacturing business as well as to restore business to a sound financial condition.

1922–
1929   Made gradual and steady progress towards financial stability through the manufacture and sale of highest grade men's fine shoes.

1929–
1930   Collapse of stock market and resulting depression found company in strong financial condition but many of its workers were out of work and others idle. General insecurity prevailed.

1931–
1934   Comparatively high shoe-factory wage rates but low annual income with resulting hardship for factory workers caused management to search diligently for a better system of worker compensation.

1935   Initiated the plan of paying workers 52 paychecks a year based on a share of production rather than wage rates and invented at the same time the drawing rate differential system.

1936   Proposed and secured approval of stockholders to placing worker representatives, chosen by themselves, on the company's Board of Directors.

1937–
1938   Share Production Plan successfully survived the economic recession and was accepted by management and workers alike as a permanent policy of organization.

1942   Appointed a member of the steering committee for the Defense Industry Advisory Committee for Shoes, Leather Products, Hides, Skins and Leather, in Washington, D.C.

1944   Initiated the classification and reserve system in connec-

	tion with the Share-Production Plan of the Nunn-Bush organization.
1947	Resigned as President of company and accepted position on Advisory Board.
1950	Retired from Company.
1951	Appointed team leader of a group of business and professional men sent by Economic Cooperation Administration (Marshall Plan) to France, Holland and Germany to conduct productivity seminars.
1953	Moved to La Jolla, California.
1953	Autobiography, *THE WHOLE MAN GOES TO WORK,* published by Harper & Brothers.
1954–1961	Continues to write, lecture and teach Human Relations in Management at San Diego State College.

CONTENTS

Part I
CAPITAL AND LABOR SHARE PRODUCTION

CHAPTER   PAGE

1. Partners in Production 3

2. Conception of the Plan 27

3. The First Exciting Years 40

4. The Plan Evolves 55

5. Labor's Compensation 62

Part II
WORKERS BELIEVE AS THEY PARTICIPATE

6. Workers Believe as They Participate 73

7. The Lot of the Worker 100

8. The Lot of Management 130

9. Shareholders and Labor 140

10. Paternalism and Welfare Plans 147

11. The Role of the Union 164

12. The New Role of Management 173

Appendices 185

Bibliography 210

Index 213

Part I

CAPITAL AND LABOR SHARE PRODUCTION

1

PARTNERS IN PRODUCTION

The Nunn-Bush Shoe Company of Milwaukee, Wisconsin, was established in 1912. The company progressed rapidly from the start, although it barely escaped financial disaster during the severe commodity depression of 1920. Since that time of crisis, the company has concentrated on the manufacture of men's fine shoes. In recent years, many manufacturers of men's fine shoes have been absorbed by such giant distributors as International Shoe Company and Genesco; the Nunn-Bush Company, however, has steadily maintained its independence. At the time of my retirement in 1950, the company had 1,100 employees in its Milwaukee plant and was doing an annual business of over 15 million dollars, which made it perhaps the largest remaining independent exclusive manufacturer of men's fine shoes in the United States.

The struggle to build democracy in this company began as early as 1915 with the extension of certain unusual rights and guarantees to all workers of three years' seniority. This initial action culminated in 1919 in a complete surrender by management of all power to make decisions unilaterally.

What today is known as the Nunn-Bush Plan first took

shape with the 52-Paychecks-a-Year-Plan in 1935. The story of the 20 years that led to the inception of the plan in 1935 and of the experiences that resulted in its further evolution are traced in detail in succeeding chapters of this book. The purpose of this chapter is to provide a concise picture of the plan as it was operating in 1950 when I left the company and as it has continued to operate, with minor modifications, ever since.*

The Concept of Democracy in Industrial Relations

At Nunn-Bush, labor and management recognize that they are partners in production, engaged in a common enterprise. Neither is considered the more important, since each is recognized as essential. Under such a concept, many matters long regarded as the exclusive prerogatives of management are recognized to be matters of common concern and interest. As such, they are decided by mutual consent, not by unilateral action.

Under this concept, the right of labor to organize and attain solidarity is not something to be accepted reluctantly, but rather to be welcomed and encouraged by management. Indeed, without some responsible spokesman representing labor, who not only can look out for labor's interests but also see that labor lives up to its commitments, industrial democracy would not be possible. Labor at Nunn-Bush is organized into a solid, independent, intramural union known as the Industrial Union of Master Craftsmen, which is recognized by management as having sole jurisdiction over all workers in the Milwaukee plant. This includes the shipping

* Although I believe I have kept myself well informed about developments since my retirement, it has seemed fairer in this chapter to present a description of the plan as I myself knew it in operation. What subsequent modifications have been made are for the most part minor or largely technical in nature and do not change essentially the picture presented here.

department workers, office workers, maintenance workers, factory workers and janitors. It does not include executives, semi-executives, foremen, and assistant foremen, who are designated as direct agents of management.

Under the Nunn-Bush Plan, management agrees by a written contract with the union that no decision affecting the workers' economic or social welfare will be implemented without the workers' sanction. The union, in turn, accepts responsibility to work toward the attainment of harmony and efficiency, and it too agrees to refrain from acting arbitrarily against management. Both parties agree in advance that if honest differences on any matter cannot be resolved successfully through consultation, they will submit the issue to arbitrators and accept their judgment. When men accept the principle of peaceful settlement and forego the use of arbitrary power, it is seldom necessary to arbitrate. Not once in 48 years has an issue had to be submitted to arbitration at Nunn-Bush.

Democracy in industrial relations involves keeping workers advised of all action at the top level and giving them a voice and a vote in decisions made. Under the Nunn-Bush Plan, the union not only has free access to the books and records of the company, but also actual voting membership on the board of directors. (Since management holds a controlling interest in the company, it is in a position to guarantee in advance the election of the representative nominated by the union.) Furthermore, the paid secretary and lawyer for the union are invited to sit with the worker director to advise him in matters on which he needs counsel.

In this manner, labor at Nunn-Bush is in position to be consulted and to make its voice heard, not only on those matters of common concern specifically defined in the contractual agreement, but also on issues usually considered the exclusive prerogative of management. To give an example, each year the board of directors fixes the compensation to be paid to officers of the company. In my experience, the worker director has never objected to the amounts approved. Had such an objection been raised while I was with the company, management would first have sought some mutually acceptable compromise and, if this had failed, would have turned the issue over to arbitration.

This part of the Nunn-Bush Plan may sound frightening to managers who have had little or no experience of working with labor on a basis of mutual trust. In practice, I have found that neither party attempts to usurp the prerogatives of the other. Each recognizes in the other, by reason of greater experience in its own field, greater competence to make certain judgments. In fixing the price of shoes, under the Nunn-Bush Plan, for example, both parties make the decision. Yet, since inception of the plan, the union representatives, although interested in the reasons for changes in prices and occasionally having expressed their opinion on the current mood of the public, have deferred to the experience and knowledge of trained merchandising men on merchandising problems.

On the other hand, while all of the rules and regulations of the factory, the work schedules, and matters of discipline are supposed also to be agreed upon mutually, in practice these matters are left largely in the hands of the workers themselves, and they have done a first-class job. For example, the union has employed a time-study and rate-making engineer trained for this job from its own ranks. Management has usually accepted his recommendations on work schedules without argument. This is what can happen when labor and management abandon the right to arbitrary action and seek to establish bona fide democracy in industrial relations.

Labor's Compensation: a Just Share of Production

It follows logically from the democratic relationship described above that the idea of labor working *for* management at some arbitrary and rigidly fixed hourly wage rate should be abandoned in favor of some plan whereby labor could work *with* management for compensation based on an equitable *sharing* of the fruits of their common enterprise. It is for this "share of production" feature that the Nunn-Bush Plan is best known. Nunn-Bush workers are paid an agreed percentage of the value they help to create, not some predetermined and rigid wage rate. The greater the total value of what the workers produce during a given year, the greater the share to be divided among them for that year. The exact amount cannot be known in advance, since the ultimate value of what is produced cannot be calculated until the quantity and price of the product are actually determined.

There is really nothing radical about this method of compensation. It is based on two principles which, while not generally recognized, have always been operative in fact. First, under any system, labor's compensation cannot for long exceed its rightful share of the actual values added to raw materials by production. If it does, there will be insufficient returns left for capital and management, and the company will fail. Second, it is not capital that pays labor's wages, but the customer who purchases the product. In a very real sense, the consumer "employs" both capital and labor, and in the long run the remuneration of both depends upon his willingness to buy their product.

In the Nunn-Bush Plan, labor and management (representing capital) agree in advance how much of the consumer's dollar will be labor's share. It is then in the interest of both parties to produce as efficiently as possible in order to compete successfully for that dollar. Labor and management automatically cooperate to their mutual profit and, eventually, to the benefit of the consumer as well. Any company willing to embrace these principles can obtain the same result. They are basic principles and apply to any industrial enterprise, although the details are certain to vary from industry to industry and may well differ considerably from the Nunn-Bush practices that will be described in detail here.

Computing labor's share. For the Nunn-Bush Company, 36½ percent of the values added to raw materials has been accepted by both labor and management as labor's just share. Statistics showed that over the years, bad and good, low prices and high, low wages rates or high, the percentage paid out in wages had remained almost constant at a little under that level. From the remaining 63½ percent come all other expenditures, including sales and promotion, taxes, maintenance expenses of all kinds, and the remuneration of management and stockholders. Although the specific percentage that goes into wages differs sharply from industry to industry, it is an economic fact that it remains constant year after year.

Under the Nunn-Bush agreement, either management or the union can request a reconsideration of this division at any time simply by giving the other ten days' notice. Any adjustment that might be made is retroactive to the beginning of the quarter in which notice is given. In theory, the provision is necessary in case some sudden, unexpected change in economic conditions should materially disturb the constancy of this ratio. In practice, neither party has ever found it necessary to call upon the short-notice provision; the infrequent changes that have been necessary have been so minor that both parties have always been content to wait until the end of a contract year to make them.

Several steps have been taken to insure uniformity of income, since it is almost as important to workers as regularity of income. In the first place, when labor's share of the value added to raw materials during each four-week period is determined (which, of course, would represent the amount to be divided), seasonal variations are leveled out by keeping a running average of the 13 preceding four-week periods and using this figure instead of actual figures for that period. This running average is obtained by dropping the figures for the oldest of the 13 periods each time and replacing them with latest figures.

Still further uniformity is obtained by basing computations on production figures rather than shipping figures, since the latter are so much more subject to seasonal variation. Seasonal variation in production is kept small, because instead of shoes being made as they are sold, production is geared to a running average of sales for the past 52 weeks—computed each week by substituting new figures for those of the corresponding weeks of the year before. Use of production figures rather than shipping or sales figures is made possible by using the wholesale prices prevailing at the time of packing as the basis for computing added values. Values of sample and trial shoes are fixed at the price prevailing on the highest custom-grade shoes produced during the same period; damaged shoes are valued at prevailing discount prices.

Drawings and reserves. The man of labor cannot wait until the books are closed at the end of each period and his share of the values created has been calculated. He needs money weekly to pay his current expenses. For this reason, a system of drawings against earnings has been devised. All workers who participate in the share-production plan are known as associates.* Each week, whether the factory works or not, each associate receives a check for ⅟₅₂ of what has been estimated conservatively as his likely annual earnings. An individual account is kept for each associate. Actual earnings are credited to his account as they are computed; drawings are deducted from it.

To provide for the possibility that drawings might exceed actual earnings, and to make drawings possible even during weeks when the factory might not be operating, each associate is required to accumulate a reserve fund amounting to 25 percent of estimated annual earnings. This reserve fund is accumulated by withholding one-half of any excess of actual earnings over drawings until such time as the reserve fund is full. On or before the 15th day of the second period following their accrual, the full amount of any excess of actual earnings over drawings is paid to associates whose reserve account is full; half of the excess is paid when a reserve account is not full. If at any time it appears that drawings are exceeding earnings at a rate that may deplete reserves below the 5 per cent level, drawings are reduced to an amount that will permit the rebuilding of reserves.

Reserves are invested in U.S. Government 2 percent F Bonds, not subject to change in value. An associate's reserve is immediately payable to him if for any reason he leaves the company. In case of his death, the reserve is paid to his executor or administrator or to his widow, according to the laws of the state. Any surplus earnings for the actual period

---

* Workers do not participate in the share-production plan until they have completed a two-year apprentice period of employment with the company, during which time they are paid hourly wages just as in any other factory. However, more than 80 percent of the factory workers are associates. A full description of the system for classifying workers is given later in this chapter.

in which he leaves are mailed to him at the same time that an accounting is given to other associates for the period in question.

If an associate is absent from work at any time that the factory is running, a proportionate deduction is made both in the amount of his drawings and in the amount of his earnings. The only exceptions to this rule are sickness, pregnancy, or emergency. In such cases, drawings may continue as long as reserves are not reduced below the 5 percent level, but earnings do not continue. This particular rule was established more at the insistence of workers than of management, for the workers have from the very first insisted that the plan should have no taint of the socialistic concept that man should serve according to his ability and receive according to his needs.

Yearly differential rates. All workers do not receive the same amount of pay at Nunn-Bush, any more than in any other factory. Under any system, some means has to be devised for differentiating between the compensation of workers according to the skill or experience required for the task performed, the disagreeableness of the task, and individual output. The hourly wage rate is ordinarily used in industry to make this differentiation. Under the Nunn-Bush Plan, yearly differential rates are set for each worker participating in the plan.

Although technically it is management's responsibility to set these individual differential rates for each associate, under the Nunn-Bush Plan they are first agreed upon cooperatively with the union. Individual rates are constantly subject to revision as the economic situation seems to warrant, or to adjustment whenever an associate changes jobs or there is some other change in his contribution to production, such as introduction of new machinery or increase of output. By agreement, no rate is changed by management without prior consultation with and approval by the union. In practice, the union has been as quick as management to demand a reduction of rate or to fine any associate whose production falls short of schedule for any length of time. There is only one exception to this system: No reduction is made in the differential rates of union officers for any loss of production that may result from time spent in discharge of union business.

An associate's yearly differential rate is not only used as the basis for determining his actual earnings, but also as the basis for setting his weekly drawings. An associate's actual earnings are his pro rata share of the total amount to be divided among participants, each of whom receives in proportion to his established rate. His weekly drawings are $\frac{1}{52}$ of his yearly differential rate. In view of this, it is interesting to note that for many years management has found it safe to fix an associate's annual differential rate at the current market hourly rate for the same individual's production at the same job times 2,080 (the number of hours in a year of 52 40-hour weeks). In other words, the return in terms of increased efficiency that has come as a result of democratic cooperation under the Nunn-Bush Plan has been sufficient to make an annual income equal to 52 40-hour weeks of work a year at prevailing rates *a safe figure for a conservative estimate of each associate's actual annual earnings.* In fact, this figure is so conservative that in some years actual earnings have exceeded it by as much as 40 percent.

Calculations for a hypothetical pay period. To illustrate how a typical associate's earnings are actually determined, let us suppose that for a given period the value of shoes packed is $1,000,000 and the cost of raw material used is $430,000. In this hypothetical case, the values added by production total $570,000. Since under the contract it is agreed that 36½ percent of the values created are to go to labor, labor's share is 36½ percent of $570,000, or $208,050.

Inasmuch as this figure represents the compensation for the entire labor force, the amount to be shared by associates cannot be determined until those who are paid on an hourly basis, instead of participating in share-production, have first been paid. If, for our hypothetical period, this amount should account for $31,207, there would then remain $176,843 as the associates' share. If, during this period, associates' drawings had totaled $126,316, there would still remain an undistributed balance of $50,527 to be divided proportionately among them.

The calculations for a typical individual are as follows: Suppose that associate Brower is performing work of a kind and quantity which would earn $2.00 an hour at prevailing competitive wage rates. His annual differential rate would be $2.00 times 2,080 hours, or $4,160; his regular weekly drawing would be ½₂ of that amount, or $80.00. If, during our hypothetical four-week period, Brower has lost no time, he will have already drawn four checks for a total of $320.00. Brower's share of the undistributed balance left after drawings is, of course, in the same proportion as his own drawings were to total drawings. Since his drawings were $320.00 and total drawings were $126,316, his share would be 320/126,316 of the undistributed $50,527, or an additional $128.02. This brings his actual earnings up to a total of $448.02 for the pay period. If Brower's reserve account is full at this time, he will soon receive an additional check for the entire $128.02. If for any reason his reserve is not full, one-half of this amount will be withheld and credited to his reserve.

Figure 1

CALCULATION: FOR TYPICAL ASSOCIATES DURING A HYPOTHETICAL
PAY PERIOD*

Value of shoes packed	$1,000,000
Cost of raw material	430,000
VALUE ADDED	570,000
Percentage to labor—36½ percent	.365
LABOR'S SHARE	208,050
Hourly wages paid	31,207
ASSOCIATES' SHARE	176,843
Associates' total drawings	126,316
UNDISTRIBUTED BAL-ANCE	$ 50,527

Associate Brower's annual differential rate is $4160; his weekly drawing is $80.00; he lost no time during the four-week period and hence has already drawn $320.00. Brower's share of the undistributed balance is 320/126,316 of $50,527.

drawings for period $320.00
due share of balance $128.02
actual total earnings $448.02

Associate Cantelli's annual differential rate is also $4160 and his weekly drawing $80.00. However, Cantelli was absent from work for two weeks during this period and hence drew only $160.00. Cantelli's share of undistributed balance is 160/126,316 of $50,527.

drawings for period $160.00
due share of balance $ 64.01
actual total earnings $224.01

Associate Martin is a slower worker than Brower or Cantelli and hence has a lower differential rate, even though engaged in the same kind of work. His annual differential rate is $3640; his weekly drawing is $70.00; he lost no time and

drawings for period $280.00
due share of balance $112.00
actual total earnings $392.00

* Because of its light work, shoe manufacture is one of the lowest paid of all industries. Government figures of August, 1959, show an average earning for workers of $57.30 per week.

hence has drawn $280.00. Martin's share of the undistributed balance is 280/126,316 of $50,527.

Associate Thomas is a less experienced worker employed at a job requiring lesser skills, and his annual differential rate is $3120; his weekly drawing is $60.00. Since he lost no time, he has drawn $240.00. Thomas' share of the undistributed balance is 240/126,316 of $50,527.

drawings for period	$240.00
due share of balance	$ 96.00
actual total earnings	$336.00

Employment and promotion policies. Under the Nunn-Bush Plan, management selects all new employees. However, each employee so hired must apply for admission into and be accepted by the union at the end of 30 days. Should the union refuse to accept him as a member, his employment is terminated at the end of this initial 30-day period. During this same 30-day period, he can be discharged summarily by management, but subsequently he can be discharged only by the agreement of both union and management.

Since it is the policy of the organization to fill vacancies in all the better jobs with workers already within the organization, new employment ordinarily is limited to inexperienced people. While an occasion will sometimes arise when management is compelled to ask the union for a temporary abandonment of this restriction, it is normally the rule. Exceptions can be made only upon mutual agreement, since it is always within the union's power to refuse to admit to membership any new employee of whom it may disapprove. In practice, this policy has created no conflict. The Nunn-Bush management has always felt that the policy promotes harmony, solidarity, and a feeling of attachment. Loyalty is a two-way street. No management can expect workers to be loyal to them unless they in turn use every means to reciprocate. This is one way to reciprocate.

Job-security provisions. One of the most important features of the Nunn-Bush Plan is its emphasis on job security. As the new worker advances step by step in seniority within the company, his degree of job security increases. Eventually, he becomes part of a permanent labor force—not subject to individual lay-off, but assured of work as long as the factory itself stays open. In advancing from the insecurity of the initial 30-day employment period to this top classification, the employee passes through several intermediate steps.

After his 30-day probationary period, during which he can be discharged by management or not accepted by the union, the new worker enters a two-year period of apprenticeship. During this time, he is classified as an "employee" and is paid at the hourly wage rate prevailing in the industry. He cannot be discharged by management, however. He can be released only by mutual agreement between management and the union. "Employees," in turn, are classified into two groups: Class "C," consisting of those under 45 years of age at the time they were hired, and Class "D," consisting of those over 45. During their two-year period as employees, no distinction is made between Class "C" and Class "D" employees.

On the first day of the first period after his second anniversary with the company, the employee is invited to become an "associate." To date, no employee has ever refused to accept associate status. Class "C" employees are then reclassified as Class "B" associates; Class "D" employees become Class "DB" associates. At this stage, no other distinction is made between them. However, this is the highest status which Class "DB" associates may attain, while Class

"B" associates may look forward eventually to achieving sufficient seniority for promotion to Class "A" status.

Promotion from Class "C" or "D" to Class "B" or "DB" brings little change in job security. Both Class "B" and "DB" members are still subject to individual lay-off in accordance with seniority if times become sufficiently slack, although not until after all Class "C" and "D" workers have been laid off first. Although the proportion of employees to associates varies from time to time, there are ordinarily enough hourly workers to insure "B" and "DB" associates much more security than the average factory worker enjoys. Since the adoption of the reserve fund plan in 1944, no associate, unless absent, has failed to draw his paycheck every week, 52 weeks a year. In fact, at no time has any associate's *drawing* even been reduced in amount, unless it was for absence when the factory was working. This is not to say that there have not been many weeks when work was so limited that *earnings* for that particular period have fallen off.

The major change that comes with advancement to associate status is remuneration. It is at this point that the hourly wage rate is abandoned; instead, the worker begins to *draw* each week ½₂ of his estimated annual income. An *employee* who has been working at an hourly wage rate of $1.75 has been receiving each week $1.75 times the number of hours worked. As an *associate*, he now draws each week ½₂ of his annual differential rate. Typically, this drawing will also amount to $1.75 an hour—but with *two* very important differences: First, as an associate he draws this amount *every week, 52 weeks a year;* second, he is credited each period with his proportionate share of all money earned by associates during the period in excess of the amount they have drawn.

Membership in Class "A" is limited to a fixed number and

can be attained only when, by seniority, a Class "B" associate has earned the right to replace a deceased or retiring "A" member. The only difference between "A" and "B" status lies in job security. "A" members constitute a permanent labor force and are not subject to individual lay-off. In slack periods, "A" members are guaranteed first call on whatever production there is up to the point that increased production necessitates additions to the labor force. If production ever should fall below this point, all "A" members share alike in whatever production there is. As necessity arises, this does not preclude slight variations in time worked by different departments or even by associates in the same department. It does preclude management's ever laying off one or more "A" members in order to give others more work.

Handicapped associates are classified as "HA" and "HB" and are men and women who were formerly "A" or "B" members but, because of some physical or mental impediment, are recognized as substandard by the Fair Labor Standard Act authorities or by the National Labor Relations Act. They are paid wages at the hourly rates approved by these authorities instead of participating in share-production as other associates do. However, they do enjoy job security identical to that of regular "A" or "B" members of comparable seniority.

"DB" members, workers above the age of 45 at the time of initial employment, are not eligible for promotion to Class "A" membership. Such discrimination may not seem justified to some. However, management and the union alike reasoned that employees serving many years in one organization were entitled to a degree of job security that could not be given to older workers who had served the most productive years of their lives with other organizations. The age of 45 seemed a fair dividing line for this purpose. In any case, most now employees customarily employed by the company were young people who had not served any other business organization for any appreciable length of time, so the "DB" class feature was used infrequently.

By contract, membership in Class "A" and "HA" is limited to a total of 620 workers. At the time I left the company, this represented something between two-thirds and three-quarters of the total labor force, excluding administration, office, and supervisory factory workers. The breakdown by classification at that time was approximately as follows:

Associates		
Class "A" and "HA"	620	
Class "B" and "HB"	135	
Class "DB"	15	
Total associates		770
Employees		
Class "C"	130	
Class "D"	10	
Total employees		140

Vacations and holidays. All workers with three months' service or longer in the factory and shipping departments receive compensation equal to their average daily earnings for the following six holidays: New Year's Day, Memorial Day, Fourth of July, Labor Day, Thanksgiving Day, Christmas Day. Workers with fifteen years of service are allowed an additional three weeks of vacation with average pay; those with between five and fifteen years are allowed two weeks; those between one year and five are allowed one week; and those over three months but less than one year are allowed one day for each three months completed.

By agreement, this compensation is over and above the basic 36½ percent of values added to raw materials by production and hence comes from capital's share. Since this vacation and holiday premium pay is just as much compensation for work performed as any other compensation received by labor, it would no doubt have been more logical to have increased the 36½ percent figure sufficiently to have included it. Such a plan even might have had the advantage of eliminating any confusion in the associate's mind about the source of pay. Like all other compensation, it comes, of course, from the man who buys the product and not as charity from a good-hearted management. However, computations would have become too complicated because of the differing lengths of vacation time.

Overtime. All employees and "HA" and "HB" associates are paid time and one-half for all time worked in excess of eight hours in any one day and for work performed on Saturdays and holidays, and double time for all work on Sundays. Since these workers are paid on an hourly basis anyway, their pay is computed under the Nunn-Bush Plan just as it would be in any comparable company in the industry. Associates, too, receive premium pay at these same ratios, both in the amount of weekly drawing and in the final accounting of actual earnings credited at the end of the period. Premium pay as finally credited amounts to time and one-half or double whatever amount actual hourly earnings for that period would have been without this overtime.

Like holiday and vacation pay, premium pay for overtime is also over and above the basic 36½ percent reserved for compensation of labor. Here a strong case can be made for paying these amounts out of capital's share. In the first place, additional production attained by working extra hours will normally bring extra profits, since overhead expenses do not rise proportionately, and labor is justified in obtaining a share of this extra profit. In the second place, the fact that labor receives this extra pay out of capital's share for overtime tends to restrain management from requiring too much overtime production, which could eventually result in the long hours and physical fatigue that labor has striven so long to eliminate.

Other social provisions. Each company in every industry has particular circumstances that require special provisions. The special provisions in the Nunn-Bush Plan illustrate its flexibility for accommodating unusual situations.

For example, because of the large demand for unskilled workers during the World War II labor shortage, abnormally large numbers of new and untrained employees left the company before they had even learned their jobs. There is always a monetary loss on inexperienced workers, and this loss is normally borne by labor as part of its share. However, under the Nunn-Bush Plan, capital interests sustain the *excess* when this loss becomes abnormal because of excessive numbers of workers leaving the company prior to completion of 65 days of employment.

Paying workers in three factory departments—sole leather, heel and counter, and shipping—posed special problems. The cutting of sole leather and the making of heels and counters are departments that some shoe factories do not have at all. Most factories buy all or some part of what they need. Since Nunn-Bush requirements varied greatly and at times many soles and heels were purchased, the company found it impractical to combine figures for these two departments with those of the balance of the factory. The irregular demands placed upon the shipping department plus the fact that it also handled materials not produced by the factory but purchased for distribution to company-owned stores created much the same problem there.

These three service departments could, of course, have

used independent figures and have been treated as independent entities. However, in view of the relatively small number of workers involved in each department, the organization decided that the disadvantage of increased accounting costs offset any advantages such a plan offered. The Nunn-Bush Plan eliminated all three departments' figures from the records and then added to the drawings of these workers exactly the same percentage of gain over drawings that associates received for the same period in the balance of the factory. Thus associates in these departments are compensated on the same proportionate basis as other associates, even though their compensation comes out of capital's share and is not charged to the share-production fund.

Capital enjoys the same benefits from the increased productivity of these departments as they do from the balance of the factory. The workers of shipping, sole leather, and heel and counter departments, closely allied with share-production workers and receiving the same material benefits of increased production, perform with the same constructive and enthusiastic spirit.

Finally, in a factory manufacturing fine shoes, no other workers have as great an opportunity to save money for the business as do those who cut fine leather shoes from the skins of small animals. Experience has shown that giving these skillful men extra incentive in the form of extra money for extra skill proves profitable to stockholders as well as to the cutters themselves. However, since the values they thus save could never be realized without the efforts of the other production workers who complete the process, the Nunn-Bush Plan by agreement with the cutters makes provision for all associates to share to some extent by crediting the workers' share-production fund with one-half of total amount earned

by cutters and the balance to the individual cutters themselves.*

The tragedy of the fixed hourly wage. At the time we were
developing the Nunn-Bush Plan we were aware that we
were making a frontal attack on two of the three great evils
that plague the free enterprise system: conflict between
capital and labor, and insecurity of employment. What we
did not fully appreciate was that we were at the same time
putting into the hands of the organization a powerful
weapon for combating the third evil, economic trade cycles.
Only slowly did it dawn on us that by eliminating fixed
hourly wage rates we had taken a long step in this direction.

Labor's compensation constitutes so large a percentage
of unit cost that when the consumer cannot or will not buy,
fixed wage rates leave the manufacturer only one choice—
to reduce production to the number of units the consumer is
willing or able to buy at present prices. They make it impossible for him to *reduce prices* to the point at which the
consumer can and will continue to buy the number of units
he had been buying previously. The tragedy of the fixed
hourly wage rate is this: The course of action that it dictates
is the one that serves only to speed and deepen the downward
cycle; the course of action that it precludes is the one that, if
the manufacturer could follow it, would slow up and eventually stop the downward trend.

The Nunn-Bush Plan avoids the tragedy that results from
fixed hourly wage rates. The company can adjust prices at
once to a changing market. If the economy is on the upgrade,
labor shares at once in the increased income without lagging
behind during a period of negotiation with a naturally reluc-

* Example: If the combined earnings of cutters for one period was $4,000,
$2,000 would be credited to entire factory share-production fund and $2,000
to individual cutters in proportion to their individual performance in cutting
leather.

tant management, which fears to fix wages higher lest the up-
swing prove only temporary. If the economy is on the downgrade, lowered prices will mean continued production without loss of jobs, even if with lowered income—a consequence
much to be preferred to the widespread unemployment and
lengthy periods of complete shutdown that result from unit
prices too high to maintain sales and hence production volume. The lesson of the Nunn-Bush Plan is plain: *Labor only
defeats its own ends by its continued devotion and misplaced
loyalty to fixed hourly wage rates.*

If the worker is going to insist on considering his labor a
commodity to be bought and sold, although this is a concept
of which I thoroughly disapprove, he could learn much from
the merchant who is an expert in the handling of commodi-
ties. When the merchant discovers the public will not buy
his goods at the price marked, he reduces the price. A good
merchant will sometimes set prices with little regard to what
goods originally cost. He considers goods worth only what
they will bring. If factory workers used the same flexibility
in their wage demands, they would soon do away with unemployment. Today's labor leadership, I fear, would view
this as a dangerous course of action, but to me it appears far
less dangerous than its alternative of heartless and pro-
tracted periods of unemployment.

Many years ago, when I was a young man in the retail
business, an experienced merchant gave me some sound advice. "In marking prices on the goods he has to sell," he said,
"a successful retailer keeps only one thing in mind—to sell
at a profit if he can, but always to sell." It took me many years
to discover that the same principle applies to successful
manufacture. I would like to see the time come when the
impediment of fixed hourly wage rates has been removed

so that every American manufacturer would be in a position
to apply this sound advice.

My long-time friend Hubert Somervell spent six weeks in
the Nunn-Bush factory in 1948 doing research for his interesting book, *Industrial Peace in Our Time*. At that time,
we collaborated in the preparation of a pamphlet describing
the share-production principle. I can think of no more ap-
propriate way to conclude the description of the Nunn-Bush
Plan than to quote briefly from this pamphlet.

> We believe in the Free Enterprise system, but we also
> believe that it can live only if we honestly recognize its
> defects and dare to apply the necessary remedies, however
> unconventional they may appear.
>
> We do not believe that a system of profit-sharing pro-
> vides the remedy for the three evils which characterize the
> Free Enterprise system—the conflict between capital and
> labor, insecurity of employment, and economic trade
> cycles.
>
> Before any improved wage structure can be introduced,
> the social and psychological problem must be faced. We
> believe that Capitalism postulates Labor as one of three
> partners in industry, Management making the third, but
> that the failure to give Labor the status of a partner is the
> basis of the whole conflict. A threefold partnership is the
> free association of three independent parties. Dictators
> contradict independence. Labor must not only be free, but
> encouraged to organize itself into an independent unit.
> It must decide equally with Management in all matters
> affecting its interests. Only so, have the other parties,
> Capital and Management, a right to expect Labor's full
> cooperation.
>
> Labor must be given its just share of the value it helps
> to create, and because we can have only what we produce,
> Labor's remuneration must be based on production.
>
> What matters to a worker is his annual income, over
> which his wage rate has no control. Annual income is con-
> trolled by production, and not by the rate at which it is
> earned. The concentration of business executives and

Union leaders alike on wage rates is, in our opinion, the biggest fallacy in much economic thought on the theory of wages.

Share the production gives workers their share of the values created. By the system of differential rates, it divides Labor's share in proportion as each individual has contributed.

Under this system, workers have neither to fight for an increase in times of rising prices, nor resist a decrease when the market falls. Their incomes keep step with business conditions. They have the right purchasing power at the right time.

2

CONCEPTION OF THE PLAN

The thinking that led to the Nunn-Bush Plan developed slowly over a period of years. In these early days, we were only dimly aware of what we were actually accomplishing and realized only in part the true potential of the plan. Gradually, through experience, we obtained insight into the full significance of what we had discovered.

The story of the Nunn-Bush Plan really starts in the early days of the depression that followed the financial crash of October 1929. By that time our company had built a large fine men's shoe business and had been making approximately 4,000 pairs of shoes per day. The men who bought them usually returned when another pair was needed.

Nevertheless, when the crisis came, a great fear gripped merchants and consumers. For a while raw-material merchants, manufacturers, and the great hordes of distributors throughout the country, both wholesale and retail, held their prices steady, hoping to save themselves from heavy losses. This unnatural situation could not last for long. Eventually prices had to come down.

Manufacturers and merchants do not like to purchase material today when they have strong reason to suspect the price will be lower tomorrow. Retail sales were declining. For every 100 pairs they had been selling, retailers were now selling about 60, and in order to reduce their inventory of high-priced merchandise, they were not ordering more than 40 replacements from the factory.

Many of our customers were out of work. They were searching their closets for old shoes and putting them back into use by having them half-soled. Not only that, but many men in those days were walking on their uppers long after they normally would have purchased a new pair.

The time came when the merchant found it futile to try to get even the cost of his merchandise. Shoes could be sold only at less than cost. Although the price of materials was coming down, wage rates, which determine labor cost, were as high as ever. Paradoxically, the worker with his wage rate unchanged found himself taking home less than half his former earnings because of reduced production.

Like many others, we thought the depression would be of short duration and that prosperity was just around the proverbial corner. We took pride in sticking out our chests and saying "if wage rates are cut, we will be the last factory in Milwaukee to do so." I believe this attitude stemmed partly from loyalty and friendship toward our workers, and partly from a feeling of guilt because of the sacrifices our workers were having to make during this period.

In the early days of the depression, our entire labor force remained at work but worked fewer hours per week. When conditions began to get worse instead of better, we asked every person in the factory who felt he could afford a vacation to take it. We said we would give him back his job as soon as business made it possible.

It was surprising how many left after this suggestion, some of them only because they realized that many in the factory needed the work more than they did. However, we still had more workers than we needed, and many of them were not earning enough to make ends meet. At such time, management has only one recourse—to lay off enough workers so that the remaining number will have sufficient work to earn a minimum living. After all efforts to induce employees to take voluntary vacations had been exhausted, we still had to lay off the 125 whom we had most recently employed. Moreover, we had to do it knowing full well that they would not be able to get a job elsewhere.

This was the most disagreeable job I ever faced in my nearly 50 years of factory experience. In the seclusion of my private office I talked with each of these men and women who had served us so well. It was not easy to look them in the eye and tell them there was no more work for them at present. But, strange to say, the dread of the job turned out to be worse than the job itself. The calm and philosophical manner of these workers, faced with such a catastrophe, was hard to understand. Instead of the criticism and self-pity I expected, they seemed to realize that I was far from enjoying what I had to do. Many said such things as "I know you can't help it, Mr. Nunn, and I'll get along some way."

When I asked them what they would do, some would say there were others in the family working. Others were going to visit relatives in the country. To each one I would reply, "If, try as hard as you can, you can't find work and the situation gets too serious, come back and see me—perhaps I can make some helpful suggestion."

I had in mind that the company would make them loans to tide them over if it was absolutely necessary, but of these 125 people only one man returned and asked for help.

During this disastrous period, all the officers, executives, and foremen, and, in fact, all salaried people, were asked to take reductions in pay. With conditions as they were, they were only too glad to do so.

By the time the depression had progressed into its third year, many of our laid-off workers had lost their homes and everything else in which they owned an equity. More and more we became convinced that some better system had to be devised. We contrasted the situation of the factory hourly wage earner with the worker on a salary. It not only seemed unfair, but also it did not even seem good business. Salaried people could be expected to be loyal, and usually were, but how could we expect factory workers to be faithful when their jobs were so insecure? A supervisor, bookkeeper, or an executive secretary had good reason to feel devotion and a willingness to give his all for a company that kept him on the payroll through thick and thin. If only one could work out some system under which a company could reasonably expect the same loyalty from machine and bench workers, what a wonderful business could be developed. Why not put workers on salaries, too?

At first thought it seemed to make sense that if we wanted bench workers to have the same attitude toward the business as salaried workers, it would be necessary to make salaried workers of them. Why not? Careful consideration of this problem soon disclosed the obstacles. We could not do so because our customers, while wearing out their shoes as fast in bad times as good, did not purchase them in like manner. If we tried to maintain the same payroll in bad years as we had in good years, there soon would have been no business. It was obvious this could not be done.

Still, I was fascinated by the idea of the worker having the same kind of security as that of salaried personnel. I was equally intrigued by the possibilities of gain for the company that such cooperation would bring.

My thoughts went back to 1915. At that time, as a substitute for the personal relationship that had existed when we were a small company, we decided to renounce certain managerial prerogatives, but only to those who had been with us for three years. As we gained confidence through experience, we gradually extended the agreement to more and more workers with increasing certainty that we had made no mistake.

Maybe we could do the same thing with this economic problem. Why not put only a small proportion of workers on salary at first, and then, as we both profited by increased cooperation, extend it gradually, just as we had slowly renounced arbitrary authority in the early years of our business? Might it not be possible to attain such a high degree of cooperation in this new and fascinating relationship that we would have nothing to fear? Surely a factory filled with men and women possessing this new kind of dignity and security would produce more, and more efficiently than seemed possible under present methods. I was convinced that factories with conventional concepts of labor would be handicapped in competing with such a business.

I discussed the matter many times with the members of the joint council* and with the business agent, as well as many other workers in the factory—cautiously at first, but each week with more assurance. To my surprise, the response was rather disappointing. If there is anyone in the world more conservative than a capitalist, it is the average worker at the bench. He fears change. Furthermore, it is extremely difficult for the worker to understand how any change that would be beneficial to the company could still be beneficial to the worker. He has been so indoctrinated with the thought

* The "supreme court" composed of eight members, four each from management and workers.

that the relationship between employers and employees is basically antagonistic, or at best one of buyers and sellers, that he believes any new system good for the buyer must automatically be bad for the seller. What is more, the worker-members on the council did not believe that the majority of the factory would accept a plan that did not put everyone on the same plane from the outset.

For the moment, I had forgotten the difference in the situations that existed in 1935 and in 1915. In 1915, the management, under an authoritarian system, could make special arrangements with a selected minority, if they chose to do so. In 1935, under a democratic system in the factory, it was entirely different. This difference between the quick decisions of an authoritarian system and the slower processes of democracy was disconcerting, but I did not give up. We were too much absorbed with the gains to be made through this kind of cooperation to drop the idea without a struggle.

I next thought of putting every worker on a salary, but stipulating in the contract that salaries could be reduced if business became so bad that such action was necessary. But how could we know when reductions in salary would be justified? And how would the worker know that such action would be fair to him? These questions caused me to go to the books of the company and find out what percentage of each dollar received had gone to the bench and machine workers. It was now the early part of 1935. Prices were low, and wage rates were lower than they had been in the boom days of the late 1920's. We went back as far as 1926 in order to include in our figures both good and bad years. The result of this investigation was astounding: Wages for the entire period averaged 19.46 percent of net sales, and—what was most surprising—the extremes varied only from 1.71 percent above to 1.28 percent below this figure.

The exact figures are given below:

1926—21.17%	1931—19.18%
1927—19.95%	1932—18.91%
1928—18.79%	1933—20.31%
1929—19.32%	1934—19.14%
1930—18.18%	

When we stopped to think that this period of 1926-1934 covered such extremes of good and bad times, high and low wage rates and shoe prices, the stability of the figures was even more remarkable. There seemed to be some little-known economic law that kept labor's share of the dollars received surprisingly constant. The total wages and the value of the product moved together like hands on a clock.

The enthusiasm with which I carried these figures and ideas based on them to my associates eventually overcame their opposition. Their only objection was that it had not been done before. I challenged all who appeared to oppose the plan to point out any possible flaw, and this they were unable to do. There was never any real opposition. Those who appeared to be opposed were only using these tactics to test my own confidence, and, after several months of discussion, they too were convinced.

However, it was an entirely different matter when I submitted the proposal at the next meeting of the joint council. The workers on the council wanted to know in detail how this new plan would work, and how the workers could be assured of the results that I so enthusiastically represented. While I was annoyed at first over their reluctance and apparent inability to grasp what seemed to me the fundamental soundness of the proposition, I could not help but understand their feelings of uncertainty about anything so new and untried.

For a long time, ever since the start of the depression, in

fact, the council had discussed the problem of unemployment, irregularity of pay, and the general insecurity of the
worker. Now at last, even though progress was annoyingly
slow, at least we could feel we were beginning to do something definite about it, as details of a plan were being evolved
in each succeeding session of the council.

We all agreed from the start that the new plan must provide a payment to the worker each week, 52 weeks a year,
even though we realized that it was not practical to guarantee the *exact amount* of this pay. We also agreed that the
new plan must give the worker more security in his job and
put emphasis on annual rather than hourly income. Although the workers fully agreed with these objectives, they
continued to ask how they could be sure payments at the
end of the year under the new plan would equal what they
had been receiving under the old system.

I realized we must find some way to reassure the workers
on this point. Finally, with the cooperation of my associates
we found a solution, and early in June 1935, made the following proposal:

Every worker of the company as of July 1, 1935, would
become an "A" member of the working force, and each of
these "A" members would participate in the new plan.

Workers employed after July 1, would be known as "B"
workers and would be paid only wages as heretofore. As "B"
members, they would also be subject to lay-off at any time
there was not sufficient work for the "A" members.

These "B" members would be promoted to "A" membership only as the "A" membership was depleted by death,
dismissal for misconduct, or voluntary withdrawal.*

Although historically the average percentage of net in-

* Because of the severe depression, total factory and shipping department
workers in the company's Milwaukee plant on July 1, 1935, numbered only 620.

come paid to workers had been 19.46 percent, we would increase the amount for the future to an even 20 percent.

Beginning on the first working day of July 1935, we would
estimate the yearly income of each worker up to July 1, 1936.
This estimate would be figured on the basis of 48 full 40-hour
weeks. It was customary to close the factory for one week of
vacation during the year. Another week was deducted for
holidays, and we estimated that two more weeks of the year
would be lost because of poor business. A worker, therefore,
would receive a check 52 weeks in the year. The amount of
each weekly check would be the amount he had previously
been paid for 37 hours of work. If our estimate of the amount
of time the factory would work proved accurate, and if there
were no change in the price of shoes, he would draw in 52
weeks practically the same amount he would have earned
under the old system. He could also expect additional compensation as increased cooperation produced increased efficiency in the plant.

In this proposal, we suggested that wage rates be called
"differential rates" under the new plan, since they would no
longer represent the workers' actual rate of pay per hour,
but instead would indicate his individual value in relation
to the other workers as a contributor to production. As such,
it would serve as the basis for calculating his portion of the
earnings.

I explained to the worker-members of the council that
having the "A" worker receive a check each week was only
part of the objective. What really mattered, I pointed out,
was what a man or woman makes a *year*. That determines
his living standard, not what he makes per *hour*. I also explained that he could not be laid off except when there was
not enough work for any of the "A" members of the company.

He would participate in all the production the company could sell.

I asked the workers on the council how, under the proposed plan, they felt about the worker who was sick, and suggested that perhaps he should get some consideration. To my surprise, the worker-members of the council were emphatically opposed to the idea. They insisted that each worker should draw according to his production. Otherwise, they argued, many workers would stay home on the slightest pretext. *They insisted that each worker should participate in earnings in the exact proportion that he contributed to production.*

Finding a satisfactory formula for supervisors posed a special problem. A plan was finally devised under which supervisors were kept at their current salaries as long as production remained at its present level. If output went up, their salaries were to be raised, but not in direct proportion to the increase. Likewise, if production should go down, their salaries were to be reduced, but again on a graduated basis.

While representatives of workers on the council were by now feeling more confident with the plan, they wondered whether the average worker in the shop was going to be satisfied to accept a reduced amount as a drawing, even though he received it every week, rather than a larger check for the weeks he worked full time. He might find it difficult at the end of a full 40-hour week not to look upon his smaller paycheck as a reduction in pay. It was easy to see that it was essential to convince each worker that the regular weekly checks he would receive in the future would be a *drawing* on account, and not *wages* for work done during that week.

In order to solve this problem, the management agreed that each worker should keep an account of the hours he worked and the amount of money he received, and, if at the end of the year he had not received at least as much under the new plan as he would have received working for an hourly wage, the company would make up the difference. Thus reassured, the worker-members of the joint council joined with the management's representatives in approving and recommending adoption of the new plan.

The management was enthusiastic over reaching this agreement in the joint council. It seemed evident that if the plan were approved by the workers, it would give our people more job security and greater regularity of pay than any factory worker had ever enjoyed before. It is true that he would not have a guaranteed salary. It was also true that he could not know for sure whether there would be work every day of the week or every week of the year, but he did have a guarantee that he could never be laid off indefinitely without cause, except when the entire "A" group was laid off for lack of work. It was anticipated also that the working force would soon be augmented by a number of "B" members, who would not enjoy the same security as "A" workers. It was reasonable to assume, therefore, that, barring a severe depression, "A" members could look forward to reasonably steady work and a paycheck every week.

We put no pressure on the workers to hurry the vote. We believed a nearly unanimous acceptance depended on everyone's having a thorough knowledge of the plan's provisions. As we discussed it week after week with the workers, we insisted they had everything to gain and nothing to lose.

Before the election, Harry Bart, president of the union, issued a pronouncement that was sent to all the workers. Dated June 4, 1935, it was headed "Going Forward":

> The straight-time plan has been discussed and analyzed from all different angles. It has been acted upon by both

committees—Shop and Council. It has been endorsed by
the business agent, and I, too, want to add a word of approval. I hope it is approved by the members.

This straight-time plan is a daring plan. Yet, it offers to
all of us financial security and something to really look forward to, just as my caption reads, 'going forward'—a progressive step. If we adopt this plan, we will be pioneering
something never attempted before; that is, straight-time
for the entire factory. It is something new and an experiment. If we are successful in operating under this plan, we
will become the talk of the shoe industry.

I want to give a bit of a pat and an orchid to the man
responsible for bringing the straight-time plan to our attention—Mr. H. L. Nunn, who is, in my estimation, the employees' true friend and counselor. With all due respect
to his associates who have cooperated with him at all
times, I use Mr. Nunn as an illustration because for years
he has been a leader, untiring in his efforts to promote
harmony, good will, and, last but not least, better working
conditions for his employees. Anyone who goes out of his
way to do this, certainly deserves praise.

Let us show our good will and appreciation towards
him and the management. How? By voting this plan in
with an overwhelming majority. It is for our own good.
Let us work as a unit, and work one for all and all for one.

HARRY M. BART, *President*
Nunn-Bush Employees Shop Union

The day came for the vote by secret ballot. It had been a
long and interesting experience. I had personally gone to
each department and talked face-to-face with our people. I
explained to each group as best I could how the plan would
work. I pointed out how increased cooperation and efficiency
could result in increased earnings for both stockholders and
workers—and most of all, I laid stress on the increased self-
respect and dignity each worker would enjoy in having more
security, more regularity of pay, and more annual income.
With 52 paychecks per year, the factory worker would be

able to make a budget and plan expenditures like salaried people.

We finished the job with no doubt about the outcome. If further argument had been needed, the clincher came as the week of July 4th approached, and with it, preparation for the customary annual shut-down during vacation week. Since it was not customary in 1935 for shoe manufacturing companies to give either paid holidays or paid vacations, under the old system employees would have received nothing, whereas under the new plan each would receive his regular drawing of 37/40 of his usual earnings for a full week of work.

The vote was practically unanimous for the plan. Yet we knew as we faced the future early in July 1935 that not all of those workers who had voted for the plan had fully understood its meaning, despite our efforts to explain it. Many, we knew, had voted as they did, not from understanding, but rather because of their confidence in us. We looked eagerly to the days ahead, convinced that these workers who had placed their trust in us would not be disappointed.

3

THE FIRST EXCITING YEARS

The new plan which the workers had accepted by secret ballot was put into the form of a contract. On July 2, 1935, officers and directors of our company and the officers and worker-members of the association council, including the business agent of the union, assembled in a small room in our recreation hall to sign the agreement. Harry Bart, president of the union, was the first to speak, and turning to me, he said:

"Mr. Nunn, I am signing this agreement with the firm belief that it represents a forward step in the relations of capital and labor. We believe it sets a pattern for all industry to follow, and I am authorized by our union to assure the company of the workers' cooperation in making the new system a big success."

Harry's formality was impressive. I can't remember his calling me "Mr. Nunn" before, but this was a solemn occasion. I believe everyone was impressed with the thought that it was an important milestone in the company's history. I tried as best I could to express the company's appreciation of the workers' confidence and to assure them we were going to do everything we could to make the plan succeed.

On July 10 the workers returned from vacation and the factory started to work under the new contract. Milwaukee newspapers had given the matter much publicity, most of it accurate. However, in the national press and magazines, the plan was often badly misinterpreted. I suppose headline writers thought it more sensational to call it a "guaranteed annual wage plan," despite our efforts to make it plain in all of our announcements and interviews that it was *not* a guaranteed annual wage. We did not want the plan thought of by the public as a rigid, fixed guarantee of some specific amount. This had been one of our objections to the old hourly rate. The flexibility of the new system was its greatest economic virtue.

The first year under the 52-Paychecks-a-Year Plan was an exciting experience. Even though much of the publicity we had received was inaccurate, the public nevertheless realized that our workers enjoyed more security than workers had been accustomed to receiving, more regularity of pay, and, most important, income calculated on an annual, rather than an hourly basis.

One could not visit our plant without detecting an unusual enthusiasm on the part of the workers. There was an alertness, an eagerness, an absence of loitering—a general activity so unusual it invariably impressed visiting factory managers, superintendents, foremen, and personnel directors. My friend, Fred Young, president of the Racine Radiator Company, after completing a trip through the shop with me, said facetiously, "I don't believe there is any such place." The time had come at last when most of the workers were acting as though they "belonged," as if it were "their" company. Some were saying with conviction "we," rather than "you."

A group of French manufacturers visiting American factories during this period expressed it in an official report, published and circulated in France, as follows:

> There is no doubt that the personnel of . . . Nunn-Bush seem at ease in the factory. They are fully aware of the community of interests, and this understanding is not only monetary. If the advantages of the two systems make a powerful bond, the motives and the state of mind that have inspired them have given birth to an understanding and a mutual sympathy really impressing.
>
> Nowhere as much as in the Nunn-Bush factory did the members of the team see the personnel breathe the joy of living with so much evidence.

With the change in worker attitude, a new and totally unfamiliar situation developed. If there were delays in receiving needed raw materials, for example, the workers wanted an explanation. If another machine was needed, the workers were impatient to get it. Why had the need for the material or the machine not been anticipated? Who was to blame? At council meetings, they investigated similar instances of inefficiency. Instead of being on the traditional offensive, management was on the defensive.

Another change occurred: Our production schedules were being met with complete regularity. The workers' committee asked management to post a production chart in each department. The workers were as interested as management in knowing what each department was doing for the common good. A worker was no longer interested only in his individual production. He was beginning to recognize that his income depended on the production of his fellow-workers as well as on his own efforts.

Workers showed a new interest in the price of our shoes. One might anticipate that workers would complain whenever prices were reduced and applaud only when they were advanced. However, I had every confidence they would never complain at taking reductions in their paychecks if it were clearly explained to them how such action would keep the factory busy and if they were reassured that their income automatically would increase as soon as circumstances justified raising prices again.

This faith proved justified. On one occasion, for example, the rise in raw-material prices led management to consider advancing our shoe prices, even though business was not good. As was the custom in such a situation, a meeting of officials was held to discuss the matter. The business agent of the union, at this time Arthur Becker, always attended meetings at which prices were discussed. Art seldom had much to say on this subject. He seemed willing to accept the judgment of those he considered more competent in the merchandising field. Like the rest of us, he was anxious to see prices increased when he was convinced such action would not hurt sales. He also understood that we should reduce prices if, by so doing, we could hope to keep up dollar volume.

On this particular occasion, he was more articulate and more positive in his attitude than usual. He said, "Gentlemen, I am opposed to raising prices at this time. I don't think people are in the mood to pay them, and it is bound to hurt sales. I know working people feel that way. The last thing I said to my wife as I left the house this morning was 'Don't you buy a goddam thing unless I know about it.'"

Art's language may have been unconventional, but we always knew what he meant, and inasmuch as we were inclined to agree with him, prices were not advanced.

Of course, some workers still had difficulty understanding how the plan worked, and one of my principal tasks was to spend time explaining it. I found one of the easiest ways to do this was to say to the worker, "It is exactly as though the

customer who buys our shoes sends us two checks instead
of one—one check, representing 20 percent of the amount
of his bill, to go to the workers, and the other check of 80
percent to go to the management to pay for raw materials,
manufacturing and sales expenses, and earnings for the
stockholders."

It was not easy, particularly for some of the younger workers, to grasp the concept of being partners in production and
not working for a wage. "Under the wage-rate system," I
would add, "you workers have always felt that labor could
never make more money through greater efficiency because
the additional profits would go to shareholders. Labor leadership, like capital, has always depended on scarcity and
restriction. Now, under our plan, you will understand that
neither shareholders nor management can gain at labor's
expense. We all profit together."

The executive board of the union consisted of one elected
representative from each of the 12 departments in the factory. These workers were selected by secret ballot, and their
president, business agent, and other officers were chosen in
the same manner. Subcommittees for special projects were
appointed by the president.

I considered it most important for the members of this
board to understand how the plan worked and how income
was divided at the end of each year. I would use large blue,
red, and white poker chips to explain how much had gone
for raw materials, how much for labor, manufacturing and
sales expenses, management, earnings, and reserves for capital.

I would then try to impress the board that the better work
we did and the finer shoes we made, the greater would be our
revenue, and the larger the share that workers, managers,

and stockholders would receive. We were all in the same boat. We were partners in production.

I explained that if the organization used more manpower than necessary, labor and capital would both suffer; management would be saddled with increased manufacturing expense—more space, machines, supervision, power, light, etc. As far as labor cost was concerned, the output of each individual was no longer a problem to management, but it was of critical importance to the workers. It would not make any difference to stockholders and management whether it required 1,000 or 500 men to do a certain amount of work, because the labor cost would be the same. But it would make a great difference to each individual worker, because 20 percent of the value of the shoes produced would be divided between those who made them, whether few or many.

We also published a chart for the workers, illustrating the division of income for the previous year (see Figure 2). Taking 1949 as an example, it showed that total sales were $14,101,644, and that, after paying for materials, fuel, transportation, distribution costs, advertising, reserves to replace plant equipment, taxes, and dividends on preferred stock, $4,999,319 remained to pay labor, management, and equity stockholders, and to provide payments for the retirement fund.

Whenever a "B" member was advanced to "A" status, I would visit him to explain the plan. After explaining the difference in wage and differential rates, I would next discuss the plan's economic implications. For instance, I would discuss the question of labor's right to some of the savings resulting from technological advances. I would explain how this principle generally has been accepted by industry, mainly as a result of pressure from organized labor. I would show how the amount of this gain is usually estimated and

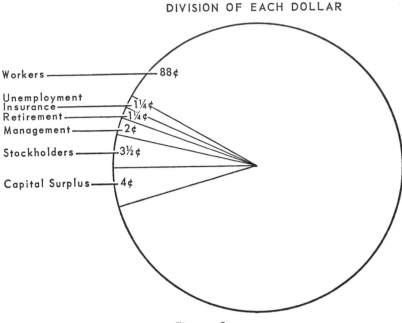

Figure 2.

provided for in long-term contracts and expressed in yearly percentages.

I would then explain how this procedure was entirely unnecessary under the Share-Production Plan, because labor profits automatically and immediately from any technological gains. I would also call his attention to the fact that to the extent competition enjoyed the same cost-reducing factors, he would have to expect prices to be cut and the public to share in the benefits of these technological advances.

Developing Scientific Rates and Schedules

As time went on, both management and the union became increasingly aware of inequalities in work schedules and differential rates. Individuals began to complain that some schedules were too lean (hard to meet) and others too fat (easy to make). With increased interest in output, all "A" members had a personal stake in seeing that no member had a schedule that was too fat.

I suggested to the union's business agent and the members of its executive board that we get a trained engineer to make a complete study of all the operations in the factory and that rates and schedules be readjusted in accordance with his findings. I pointed out that management would derive no special benefit, since although changes in differential rates would affect the individual worker's earnings, they would in no way affect management's share. Management's share was fixed at 80 percent of value of production. The workers' share was the remaining 20 percent, and it was in their interest to see that their portion was distributed as equitably as possible.

The workers' executive board appreciated this point, but they had never before had anyone in the factory with a stop-watch. Each person was afraid that the timing of his operation might result in his having to work faster than he had been working at his present differential rate.

After the pro's and con's of hiring an engineer had been discussed for some time, the business agent made a suggestion. If the management would agree to the union's having one of their men work with this engineer and see exactly how he arrived at his figures, they would be willing to try it out. So we employed an experienced industrial engineer, and the workers selected Billy Loppnow, a young man from the factory, to work with him. Billy had a mathematical mind. It was remarkable how quickly he learned the intricacies of a slide rule. Working together, these men made many recommendations for changes in schedules. As long as the workers, acting through their Executive Board, approved the changes, management was satisfied.

Because business was good and production rapidly increasing, new "B" members were being added to the working force; and, as the "A" membership was depleted through death or retirement (it was a rare exception for "A" workers to leave for any other reason), their place was taken by the "B" member with the highest seniority.

The "A" members were not slow in realizing that "B" class workers were literally working for them, even though being directed by management. Consequently, the attitude toward the new employee changed. Under a conventional wage system, a worker who could soldier on the job and get away with it was considered smart. Workers were generally amused, rather than aggravated, at the discomfiture of the supervisor. This was no longer true. A "B" member's production was watched by his fellow workers in "A" class. If he did not earn what he was being paid, he would be reported to the business agent of the union and soon put in his place. The workers' business agent was as much concerned with production as was management.

By January 1, 1936, after the 52-Paychecks-a-Year Plan had been in effect six months, the workers had received a check each week plus an additional 5 percent. This adjusted compensation resulted from an increase in prices and sales, as well as in efficiency. At this same time, since it appeared that the increased prices and sales would continue throughout the months ahead, the multiplier was increased from 37 to 40. In spite of this increase of 8 percent in the drawing accounts, the "A" workers earned during 1936 additional compensation of 4.8 percent above their drawings. On May 1, 1937, all differential rates were increased 5 percent, and during 1937 each class "A" worker averaged 5.2 percent over his regular drawings.

About July 1, 1937, business began to drop off, and we had to work some short weeks. The drawings of "A" workers began to exceed the earnings, and instead of a surplus to distribute to "A" workers, there began to be a deficit. However, we thought the lull in business would be of short duration. Rather than ask the workers to reduce the differential rate or the multiplier, we told the shop committee that as long as they would make up the deficit later, we would not insist upon our right to reduce the drawings, as we could have done under the contract.

The deficit had risen to more than $50,000 by the first of the year, and management belatedly asked that a reduction be made in drawings. Therefore, on January 17, 1938, all differential rates were reduced five cents. A short time later, it became apparent business was getting worse rather than better, and the multiplier was reduced to 37, placing the drawings on the same basis they were during the first six months of the original contract. This last reduction brought drawings below earnings and the deficit slowly but surely was being reduced. The workers' attitude was splendid. I can well remember a remark made by Arthur Schwanburg, a member of the executive board of the union: "We have had some good years under the plan—let's show people we can be good losers now and repay what we have overdrawn."

An interesting thing occurred during this period of depression: Class "B" members were retained, even though under our contract they could have been laid off. The "A" workers insisted upon doing the generous thing by dividing the work with class "B" members. At this time there were 89.3 percent class "A" and 10.7 percent class "B" members.

Outsiders had said in the early days of this new relation-

ship that it would work all right while prices were going up,
but it would be another matter when prices started going
down. If these skeptics could have witnessed the cooperation
we received during the six months of declining prices, they
would have changed their minds. Workers can give as well
as take, and it has been my experience that they do it with as
much grace as does the average businessman.

We had now experienced bad as well as good times, and
both the management and workers were satisfied with the
way the plan had worked. We discovered that we had accomplished something more than giving the workers added
security, greater regularity of pay, and higher annual income. The management began to realize that in seeking to
satisfy these needs of our workers we had found something
of vital importance: Capital and labor had a common interest. Were we not both seeking the same thing from the same
source—capital supplying the plant and tools and financing
the operations, while labor processed the raw material? After
all, I reasoned, capital and labor can divide only what is left
after raw material, overhead, and sales expenses are paid.
For instance, if these items take 75 cents out of each dollar
we receive, we can divide only the 25 cents left. Such being
the case, why not call the plan Share-Production, rather than
52-Paychecks-a-Year, which seemed to imply the old relationship of capital buying labor?

In the fall of 1938, I had suggested to my management
colleagues that the stockholders of the company ask the
workers in our retail stores and departments (consisting at
that time of approximately 150 men) and the workers in our
factory each to nominate a candidate for the company's
board of directors. Since the majority of stock was owned by
people connected with the business (total stockholders at
the time I retired from the company numbered approxi-

mately 600), all we had to do to assure these store and factory nominees election to the board was to amend our charter
to provide for seven instead of five directors.

I was surprised and delighted at the absence of any opposition to my proposal. The success of our Share-Production Plan had made the sales as well as production forces of
the company so enthusiastic that they were only too eager to
approve any proposal that promised increased understanding and cooperation.

Theodore Kuecker, assistant general retail store manager,
was nominated by the Retail Store and Department Division,
and Gus Kreckle, a highly respected Goodyear stitcher, by
the factory. These men were elected and sat at their first
board meeting in January 1939.

It is true that the average machine operator is not likely
to be informed on many things that come up during a director's meeting of an industrial organization, nor does his
experience qualify him to participate in the discussion on
many matters on which decisions have to be made. However,
it is not unusual for boards to include men of limited knowledge about the business. A banker, for instance, can be helpful when it comes to discussing financial matters, but he may
have absolutely no knowledge of factory problems.

The worker-director was deeply interested, and he learned
many things. His greater knowledge of the attitudes and
thinking of the workers supplied the board at times with
information they would never have received otherwise. This
worker was invariably a good listener, and he left the meeting with a greater realization of the problems and responsibilities of officers and directors.

Inasmuch as our officers drew moderate salaries for work
of such responsibility, I believed it would be helpful in our
efforts to secure mutual trust for our workers to know the

exact figures. I also wanted them to know that there were no secret schemes being concocted behind closed doors and drawn curtains that might be inimical to the workers' interests.

Believing in the advantage of friendship and trust between management and labor, I wanted our management to do everything possible to inspire our workers also to strive for this same objective.

For instance, before that directors' meeting in January 1939 when worker-representatives first sat on the board, and when officers' salaries were to be considered, I discussed the matter with worker-director Gus Kreckle. I said, "Gus, we will be setting the officers' salaries at this meeting, and I have an idea that you may be shocked when you learn that Mr. Bush and I, who have been drawing the highest salaries, will ask for about four or five times as much as the highest paid machine worker in the factory." "No," Gus replied, "I know the big bosses always get big money." "But, that is not the point, Gus," I replied, "What I am saying is, is it too much? We are not going to be arbitrary about it. We expect to receive only salaries that are consistent with our talent and experience and commensurate with the responsibility we carry and the record we make as good managers. I appreciate you may not have much of an idea how to evaluate this kind of service, and this is one of the reasons you should bring John Waddleton (workers' paid secretary and counsel) with you to the meeting. He is posted on these matters, and I am sure he will never advise you to vote for excessive salaries. And let me add, Gus," I continued, "I will never ask for a salary that you as the workers' representative—after careful investigation—believe is excessive, and I am sure the other officers feel the same way. Not because we would not enjoy more money, but because we believe that in the long run we will have a sounder business and make more money if we can earn and enjoy the workers' confidence in our fairness."

It is a matter of record that the workers' counsel assured Gus at the meeting that the officers' salary schedule was moderate and advised him to vote with capital's representatives to approve it.

It is a wholesome influence on men of power to have at the board table representatives of the men and women in factories and stores—so economically weak as individuals, but so strong and powerful as a group; a force that can be so destructive, if ignored or misled, but so helpful and cooperative if recognized and made an integral part of the organization.

The executive board of the union evolved a significant labor policy in connection with this new privilege of having a worker representatve on the company's board of directors. The workers' board was so eager to have good and competent representation and so fearful that many workers would not realize its importance that its members decided that the board should nominate workers whom they considered qualified. From this list, they would ask the workers to vote for their choice. They felt that this would insure the selection of a well qualified man—mature, experienced, and deliberative.

Their action reminded me of the shop committee* of the old association, who always used good judgment in selecting members of the joint council. The shop committee itself might have many members of a contentious and uncooperative nature, but their selections for the council would invariably be men of maturity and conservatism.

---

* Subsequent to the passage of the National Labor Relations Law in 1935, known as the Wagner Act, the Nunn-Bush organization had, in addition to a shop committee elected by the workers, a joint council of eight members, four members chosen by the shop committee and four by Nunn-Bush management.

Our constant campaign to help all the workers understand the principle of mutuality of interest slowly but surely achieved its purpose, and the time came when there were few "A" workers who did not grasp the fundamentals of the plan. Some may not have been able to explain it to others, but nevertheless they had at least learned that their pay was fluctuating according to value of production and that they were not being given bonuses.

4

THE PLAN EVOLVES

The first important change in the Share-Production Plan came in January 1939. It was a result of the lessons we learned during the period when we were reducing the deficit that we had incurred in the fall of 1937, when drawings had temporarily exceeded earnings. Although our workers had cooperated splendidly in agreeing to smaller drawings in order to reduce this deficit, as time dragged on I could sense an understandable impatience on their part. I realized that some step should be taken to prevent the organization from ever again facing any such long period spent in reducing a deficit.

The most practical plan was to build up a reserve while earnings were high, so that drawings could be made against it whenever earnings were reduced temporarily. I therefore went to the executive board of the union and said, "Management hopes that you have come to the same conclusion that we have—that deficits are bad and surpluses good. We can now see very plainly, as we hope you can, that during the good days of the plan, instead of your drawing all those extra checks, some of that extra money should have been left in a surplus fund to take care of the hard times that always come.

It is easy to see now that if we had done that we would never have been forced to reduce the differential rate or multiplier.

"We would like to propose, then, that in the future each worker carry a reserve of not less than 5 percent of his estimated annual income. In other words, each of you would not draw any adjusted compensation until you had built up your 5 percent reserve. After that has been provided, you would of course draw your entire earnings, just as you have been doing." As a gesture of cooperation and to avoid prolonging the period of reduced income for the workers, the company further proposed at the same time to write off the small remaining balance of the existing deficit, at that time approximately $15,000. The workers readily accepted this amendment to the plan. In fact, it was not long before growing awareness of its value led them voluntarily to propose an increase of the reserve to 15 percent. It was later increased to 25 percent, and still later to 35 percent.

In 1942, a classification system was adopted. New workers were classified as "C" or "D," and the period to be served as an "employee" before beginning to share in production was set at two years. At this time, the term "associates" was adopted to designate those workers participating in the Share-Production Plan.

During the second World War, the plan operated so smoothly that no further changes were necessary. In fact, our associates found themselves in a particularly favored position during this period. Prices of shoes and wages were fixed for all companies, but since Nunn-Bush associates did not work on a wage-rate basis, they could still obtain increases in income through their share in any gains that might result from increased efficiency. Thus, while other companies were complaining of insufficient labor or apathy on the part of workers because of the great demand and the fixing of wage rates, Nunn-Bush was able to maintain both the quality of the shoes produced and the amount of production. Both worker and capital interests profited accordingly.

In 1946, the next development in our plan evolved from our desire to bid on goverment army shoes of a comparatively simple nature. The amount of labor needed to make this shoe was less than required for our regular average production. In order to be competitive in our bidding, we therefore secured from the executive board of the union their consent to reduce labor's share on government shoes from 20 percent to 19 percent.

We secured a contract for these shoes and decided that, although a factory making a single product could without difficulty reflect the right share of labor with a constant figure, it might be better and more equitable if we grouped our various types of shoes according to man-hours of labor required and put a different percentage for labor on each group. After all, we were making more than one grade of shoe, and many types in each grade. Some shoes were plain, others had a great deal of ornamental stitching. Some styles had difficult patterns, others had simple ones. Variations of this kind occurred in each department.

In past years, the proportion of complicated patterns to simple styles sold remained remarkably constant. The consistent ratio of labor cost to price of shoes that we had found when we developed our first figures had clearly shown this. But now we were having complaints from the union's executive board that difficult patterns and shoes with ornamental stitching were on the increase. Since it was inevitable that demand would change from year to year, I felt the company would be in a stronger competitive position on staple shoes if we introduced a graduated scale of percentages for labor, keeping the over-all average at the same 20 percent we had been using since 1935.

Plain, simple types, which constituted the great majority, were therefore placed at the same percentage we had agreed upon for army shoes, 19 percent. More complicated types were assigned labor percentages varying from 20 to 26 percent, depending on the man-hours needed.

Another change came soon after the end of World War II. It had been in my mind since I had first learned about the ideas of A. W. Rucker late in the 1930's. Rucker advocated basing labor's share on the values added to raw materials rather than on total sales as we were doing. The figures that had originally shown that labor's share of sales price had run slightly under 20 percent also disclosed that labor costs had approximated 36 percent of value added to raw materials. On this phase of the plan, Rucker's ideas seemed sounder than ours, but both the workers and my associates in top management had been reluctant to discuss such a change when the plan was working so well.

At the end of the war, the clamor for removal of trade restrictions became so great that in 1947 price controls were removed. The price of many raw materials required in the manufacture of men's shoes advanced 100 percent practically overnight. A few simple calculations quickly showed that because of our failure to adopt the added-value concept earlier, we were now in trouble.

Let us look at a typical example. When the cost of raw materials for a given pair of shoes was $3.56 and the wholesale price of these shoes $8.00, it had made no difference whether or not labor's share was figured as 20 percent of $8.00 (as we had been doing) or at 36 percent of $4.44, which was the value added to raw materials (computed by

subtracting $3.56 from $8.00). In either case, labor's share
was $1.60 per pair.

However, after controls were removed, the cost of raw
materials for the same pair of shoes rose suddenly to $6.23.
If we were to remain competitive, we could not raise the
wholesale price of these shoes above $12.50. Figured at 20
percent of $12.50, the formula we were actually using, labor's
share now became $2.50. However, 36 percent of $6.27
($12.50 minus $6.23) would have given labor only $2.2572
—almost 10 percent less. To express it another way, under
the formula we were using, labor was now receiving approximately 40 per cent of added value instead of the 36
per cent that had previously been determined as its correct
share.

To change the method of figuring labor's share would be
equivalent to asking the workers to accept voluntarily a 10
percent reduction in pay. If it were not changed, we would
have to meet all other obligations out of only 60 percent of
added values instead of the customary 64 percent—something that could not be done if prices were to be kept competitive. As I had done on other crucial occasions, I decided
to present the facts to the workers face-to-face.

This time, instead of going into each department, I wanted
to talk to the entire factory at one time. The union was due
to have a regular meeting in the recreation hall, and I had
no difficulty in getting permission to speak.

I first reviewed the history of the plan from the beginning—the reasons back of its conception, the added security
and regularity of pay for workers that we hoped to accomplish, and the research that we had done in finding that
the workers' share in the dollars produced had been constant
over the preceding years. After describing the research of
A. W. Rucker, I explained how several years before I had

tried to convince others in the organization that we should make the change from a percentage of total values to a percentage of values added to raw material, and how, since we had been doing so well, it was decided to leave well enough alone. Now, the sudden phenomenal rise in prices of raw material had upset the apple cart. While the workers were enjoying the fruits of greatly advanced prices, the stockholders, if something were not done, would actually be obliged to accept reduced returns. No plan could succeed on that basis. What was good for one must be good for the other. The plan as it was then constituted would never have been successful if it had not been beneficial to both. I reviewed the figure since the inception of the plan: each associate for the 12 years since July 3, 1935, had drawn a check every week, the least of which had been as much as it had been at the beginning of the contract, and most of which had been much more. In addition to this, I pointed out the great number of additional checks for surplus over drawings that had been received at the end of each month.

Admittedly, the proposed change would mean an immediate reduction in income of about 10 percent, but it would restore the plan to a sound basis. I did not believe that the workers wanted anything that was not sound and that was not fair. I called attention to the fact that the whole country had been interested in our experiment, and that many had said workers will take, but they will not give. I had always emphatically denied that such was the case. Here was an opportunity to prove me right, and I had complete confidence that they would do so by a resounding majority. I spoke for about an hour. You could have heard a pin drop. There was only polite applause when I finished, but every face turned toward me. I had a feeling that each was trying hard to understand the issues involved and to determine how he should vote.

The secret ballot was taken the following day, and the proposition to change the plan was carried by an overwhelming majority. These workers, by secret ballot, had voluntarily accepted approximately a 10 percent reduction in their income because they were convinced it was the fair thing to do and that the plan itself might be endangered if it were not done.

There have been a few further slight changes in the plan since I left the company in 1950. For one thing, the percentage of added values allocated to labor has been increased to 36½ percent. There have been some minor changes in the relations between management and workers, and there will undoubtedly be more changes as experience dictates.

I am convinced of one thing: as long as there are any of the original group of management or workers, the following two basic principles, cornerstones of industrial democracy, will never be abandoned:

1. The principle of the community of interest of both labor and management in the success of the enterprise, and the recognition that this success depends upon their mutual, cooperative effort.

2. The principle of settlement of all disputes by judicial or semi-judicial processes, and the voluntary abandonment by all parties of the right to arbitrary, unilateral action.

5

LABOR'S COMPENSATION

We at Nunn-Bush were not the only ones to recognize the wage-rate fallacy and to realize that labor can hope to receive only a fair share of the wealth it produces.

As early as 1932, Allen W. Rucker, president of the Eddy-Rucker-Nickels Company (Cambridge, Massachussetts) and a practical business economist, became convinced that "industrial growth in the United States was being hampered by misdirected attempts both through collective bargaining and legislation to raise income and cure unemployment by manipulating hourly wage-rates and working hours." He believed such efforts ignored the underlying principles of labor compensation. He had discovered after much research that, regardless of the level of wage-rates or prices, whether the economy was on the upgrade or downgrade, *total wage payrolls had remained an almost constant percentage of the value added to raw materials by the manufacturing process.* He concluded that labor could achieve a higher standard of living only by raising total income through higher productivity.

Rucker's company published a pamphlet in 1934 entitled *Pay as you produce plan.* This was followed in 1937 by a book

entitled *Labor's road to plenty*. In 1952, Rucker published
*Progress in productivity and pay—All U.S. Manufacturing
Combined*. The Rucker Share of Production Plan has been
installed since 1937 in many organizations both in the United
States and in foreign countries as well.

While Rucker considers the wage-rate as only a differential wage-rate and one of the "great inventions of industrial
civilization because it determines the proper compensation
differentials between the differing skill and merit of individuals," he also considers its misuse as "one of the greatest
tragedies of industrial civilization." To Rucker, "two basic
principles (rather than merely one) of compensation are
(1) the differential wage-rate for compensation of individuals, and (2) the proportional share of production values
for compensation of labor as a whole." He also says "the
hourly wage-rate is not an income, but merely the rate at
which income is earned."

We at Nunn-Bush knew nothing of the Rucker Plan in
1935, when our 52-Paychecks-a-Year Plan was inaugurated.
Indeed, at that time we were concerned entirely with the
problems of our own company—with job security and
regularity of income for our own workers. Rucker, on the
other hand, as an economist and a management consultant,
was concerned with the national economy. The economic
objectives of the two plans, however, were quite similar.

Both the Rucker and Nunn-Bush plans emphasize how
deceptive and misleading other methods of expressing income can be. Since both plans (Nunn-Bush since 1947)
divide values added to raw material rather than the sales
dollar, both provide incentives for saving material, for reducing the number of rejects, and for good workmanship in
general. The Nunn-Bush Plan has the added value for workers (and for management and stockholders too, in the long

run) of added security of employment for "A" workers, uniformity of pay (by reason of the company averaging values of production month by month) and, most important of all, regularity of income through operation of drawing accounts (rather than rigid wage-rates) and associate reserves.

The national and international publicity that the Nunn-Bush Plan received aroused much interest on the part of industrial managements. Many of them sent representatives to investigate, and many vainly endeavored to enlist the interest of their labor force. One company only, of the hundreds we welcomed—The Scott & McHale Shoe Company (London, Ontario, Canada)—sent a delegation of *workmen* (selected by their own labor force) to visit their brother *workmen* in our plant.

In 1938, this company installed the same type of plan they had seen in our plant, basing worker's income on a percentage of total value of sales and using the device of a flexible weekly drawing account. It is significant that this company, which, like Nunn-Bush, has surrendered all arbitrary managerial prerogatives, has also enjoyed continued peace and prosperity.

In 1938, the Adamson Company, a steel company located in East Palestine, Ohio, found itself in serious financial difficulty. A representative of the company and several labor leaders in the steel industry, including Joseph Scanlon, called on Clinton S. Golden, then vice-president of the Steelworkers' Union. Golden, who understood the mutuality of interests of capital and labor and who had for some time advocated cooperation, urged them to try to work out some plan that would save the business for the stockholders and save the jobs for the workers. The cooperative action thus initiated by Scanlon and Adamson resulted in a lowering of labor costs for Adamson and increased compensation for the workers. This was an advanced step in the relations of an industrial management and a national labor union.

As a result of this experience, Joseph Scanlon developed what has come to be known as the Scanlon Plan. First installed at the Adamson plant in 1945, it was later accepted by the Lapointe Machine Tool Company (Hudson, Massachusetts) in 1947, and since that time has proven successful in many plants, thanks to the enlightened vision and leadership of its founder. Usually it has been introduced after an experience of acute conflict, often between unorganized labor and management. Sometimes a union organization would emerge from the conflict, and sometimes relations would become so strained and bitter as to threaten the survival of the company. In such a climate, someone, either in the union or the management, would take the initiative to find a solution. It was usually under such circumstances that the Scanlon Plan would be adopted as a means of survival of the business.

Scanlon had knowledge, sympathy, and an understanding of the worker that aided him greatly in his work. Understanding as he did the potential of the working man, he appreciated the possibilities inherent in cooperative efforts. In developing a formula that compensates the working force fairly for increasing production, without putting an added burden on a business already staggering in its efforts to make ends meet, he sought to utilize the worker's superior knowledge of his particular job. The way to reduce labor costs, Scanlon concluded, was to make use of this special know-how possessed by the working force.

Scanlon believed that collective bargaining, as practiced generally by industrial management and organized labor, was a primitive affair. The real objective of both management and workers, he felt, should be the development of a more "mature relationship" that could make full use of the special knowledge and abilities of both. The worker-management cooperative plan that he first introduced in the Adamson plant provided that workers would get a bonus if and when labor costs were reduced below past normal experience. Labor costs, however, were not expressed in terms of wage rates, but of the percentage of the value of production that total wages and salaries constituted. Thus the Scanlon Plan is based upon labor's receiving a share of production based on value of sales (similar to that phase of the original Nunn-Bush plan), while the Rucker Share of Production Plan is based on labor receiving a percentage of values added by manufacture to raw material, which, as I have already stated, we considered a sounder basis of arriving at labor's rightful share.

The Scanlon Plan required management to withhold 25 percent of any gain over the norm in order to build a surplus to protect the company in the event that there should later be months when the workers' pay exceeded the norm. After this 25 percent was put in reserve, the balance would be split, with 25 percent going to the company and 75 percent being paid out as a cash bonus to participants in the plan. This division of the earnings over the norm was a matter of negotiation. Some companies using the Scanlon Plan give the workers 100 percent of all gains over the norm.

I have been impressed with the amount of cooperation that it has generated in many companies. However, none of the companies using either the Rucker or the Scanlon Plans have adopted the provisions that make the Nunn-Bush and Scott-McHale systems substantially different in terms of job security, regularity of pay, and capacity for adjusting to deflation through flexibility of compensation. Neither the Rucker Plan nor the Scanlon Plan pretend to come to grips

with the problems of arbitrary action by unions or managements.

No system of compensation, regardless of whether it is
the simple payment of a wage-rate per hour with or without
additional incentive payments of bonus or profit-sharing, or
a share-production system, based either on a share of sales
or a share of values added to raw materials, is complete unless it contains agreements that make possible quick reduction of labor cost when prices are weak and demand is declining as well as advances when prices are rising. Without
such agreements, no plan provides the essential flexibility
found in the Nunn-Bush Plan. Unless this additional step is
taken, companies using share-production systems and retaining the orthodox manner of paying labor a fixed wage per
hour or per piece (other than provided by law) maintain
much of the buyer-and-seller concept of capital and labor
relationship. It leaves untouched the revolutionary potential
of the Nunn-Bush Plan for keeping our economy in balance.

It is not my intention to indict the contributions of either
Rucker or Scanlon. In all fairness, it must be pointed out that
there is nothing inherent in their system *per se* that necessarily requires the perpetuation of a rigid buyer-seller concept. Both plans have proven to be sound and successful
economic incentives and are well designed for organizations
that have not developed sufficient mutual trust between
management and workers to take the complete step of aban-
doning entirely the fallacious wage-rate system. Every system initially has to work within the limits of conditions as
they exist. Even Nunn-Bush, favored with a long record of
amiable labor relations, found it advisable in the *beginning*
to guarantee that labor's share of production would not be
less in dollars than labor would have earned for the same

number of hours worked on a wage-rate basis. However, after the first year the workers never raised the point again.

Both the Rucker and Scanlon Plans, it seems to me, provide a fine foundation for developing the teamwork out of which eventually this necessary mutual confidence and trust can emerge. It is not my intention to criticize either plan, but merely to point out that organizations adopting them should look forward as early as possible to the day when they too can take this desirable additional step forward and attain the cost and price flexibility that comes when the rigid elements are eliminated.

It should be kept in mind that Rucker and the Scanlon Plans have been installed in many organizations that are concerned only with job-shop business, in companies producing exclusively seasonable merchandise, and in companies producing products that are not practical to warehouse. Obviously, it is more difficult to provide such workers with such uniform and regular drawings as does Nunn-Bush; but even so, it is my contention, the worker needs more uniform and regular pay, regardless of how irregularly he earns it. I also contend that it is possible for any organization adopting the share-production principle to abolish rigid wage-rates and substitute in their place a flexible differential drawing system. Even more important for his greater annual income, as well as the best interests of management and stockholders, is the opportunity management is given, when not saddled with rigid wage-rates, to quickly reduce prices of their merchandise on a declining market.

Sharing production, as practiced by Nunn-Bush, is not a system applicable only to shoe manufacturing or other production types of business. The plan has to be tailored to fit the needs of each particular business. There will be no failures where management and men have mutual trust and the will and determination to find the solution.

After retiring from the Nunn-Bush Company on October 31, 1950, I reflected with pride on the circumstances that had enabled us to build an exceedingly prosperous shoe manufacturing business. It was also gratifying to realize that, through cooperation with our faithful workers, we had built a system that had enabled them as well as stockholders and management to share in this prosperity.

We had attained an enviable reputation among the shoe dealers of the country, and such a reputation is not easy to secure in the field of high-grade men's shoes. Shoes are not like food or many kinds of wearing apparel, whose merits can be determined quickly. Men with the means to buy the best are extremely slow to change after finding a brand of good appearance, wearing quality, and comfort.

The success of the Nunn-Bush Shoe Company can be attributed to many things. At the birth of the company, the management was young but experienced and had a firm determination to succeed. Both the sales and the accounting departments were in the hands of men of ability, energy, and integrity. The company's standing in the raw-material market and its credit in the financial institutions were exceedingly high. All these factors unquestionably were essential to the company's success.

Our company's unique asset was its discovery of a policy that developed a remarkable degree of *human cooperation*. The making of shoes entails several hundred different operations, the great majority of which are simple and easy to learn. Nevertheless, they are all important, and the quality of the finished product depends on each individual worker's efforts. The spirit of cooperation in the Nunn-Bush factory developed the pride and self-respect that led each worker to perform his task just a little more conscientiously.

I am convinced that much of the success of the company can be credited to this extra care in workmanship. In the long run, it was this consistently fine quality that appealed to the customer who bought our product and continued to buy it. After all, in a very real sense every company, management and worker alike, works for and is paid only by the consumer who buys its product.

Part II

WORKERS BELIEVE AS THEY PARTICIPATE

6

WORKERS BELIEVE AS THEY PARTICIPATE

I had never questioned the proposition that labor was only a commodity to be purchased as cheaply as possible until one day in 1908. I was showing Tom Drew through the plant, preliminary to his going to work as the new foreman of the Bottoming Room of the Cape Girardeau factory of the Roberts, Johnson & Rand Shoe Co. (St. Louis, Missouri).

With a great deal of pride, I called his attention to how much work a certain shoemaker was doing and the wage we paid for it. Drew turned to me with a look of incredulity on his face as he said, "But Mr. Nunn, how can the man live on so little?"

Never before had I been asked such a question. On the contrary, I had invariably listened to words of praise and astonishment at our ability to get so much for so little. Did Drew think there was any responsibility on our part to pay this man any more money than we had to? I had never heard of such a thing. He did not have to work in our factory if he did not like the wages. Let him work somewhere else!

But, even so, I could not forget Drew's frank and accusing words, "How can the man live on so little?" The observation burned into my consciousness.

During the five years prior to this incident, I had served as office-manager, foreman, and for the previous three years, as superintendent of the Hickory Street factory of the same company in St. Louis. I had succeeded in building a reputation for making shoes at a low cost, and I had organized the Cape Girardeau factory with the firm determination to add to that reputation.

This incident concerning Tom Drew has always seemed to me to be the turning point in my social consciousness. During a two-year leave of absence because of illness, beginning shortly after my talk with Drew, I had time to do a lot of thinking. While no definite plan was developed, I did conceive a hazy vision of some improved relationship between management and labor that would result in a better reward for labor—not only in increased wages, but in added self-respect and dignity. However, along with my new regard for the welfare of employees, the thought always persisted that management and stockholders *also* would be rewarded by increased cooperation of labor that such an improved relationship would bring.

Such thinking was, admittedly, still tainted with the same devotion to self-interest that I always had. Yet, the thought of a plan that would allow the other fellow, as well as myself, to enjoy increased prosperity seemed an advance over the kind of labor exploitation that had existed at Cape Girardeau.

Returning to work in 1910 after my long inactivity, I decided to cast my lot with my old friend Harsh, the man I had succeeded at Hickory Street and who had in the meantime started his own business in Milwaukee, Wisconsin.

Harsh was as authoritarian in his thinking as a Prussian general. He frustrated every attempt I made to alter the traditional relationship between management and workers.

There were too many restraints. In the summer of 1912, I persuaded two former associates of mine in St. Louis, A. W. Bush and M. V. Kedian, together with my banker brother-in-law, W. E. Weldon, to join me in organizing the Nunn & Bush Shoe Company (later changed to Nunn, Bush & Weldon Shoe Company, and still later to the Nunn-Bush Shoe Company, the title the company now bears).

There were no labor problems in the formative years of the new company. I personally hired all the factory workers and, with the help of a few assistants, directed their work. I also did the disciplining, as well as discharging, when necessary.

We had a friendly relationship with the first small group of about one hundred men and women. It was much as it had been in the first department I had supervised at Hickory Street, except that I had no pressure from above. All tension was removed. It might have remained that way, too, if three things had not happened—two external, and the other internal. Our business was growing fast, and I was frequently compelled to leave the city in order to call on the jobbing trade. This, together with our rapid growth, compelled me to hire foremen for the various departments and give them the authority such responsibility required.

For the first time since we started our business, foremen gave the orders to the workers. I began to lose that direct contact that had always given me a sense of security. The resulting insecurity was aggravated by the news, one day, in the spring of 1914, that a union organizer was in the city and was fast signing up the workers of the various shoe factories for membership in his radical union.*

So far as we knew, he had left our little shop alone. After he had called a strike in the large Milwaukee shoe factories,

* Not affiliated with American Federation of Labor, or other association of unions considered responsible in those days.

however, we could sense an understandable unrest among our people. Their fellow workers were on the street with no pay, and they were working and making no sacrifice for the cause. Some of the leaders in the factory were wondering if they should join in the strike to show their sympathy. As soon as I learned of this, I went out into the shop and asked the workers to gather around. The power to the machines had been turned off and all the workers were still and quiet. I told them I knew perfectly well what they were thinking about and that I did not consider it *my* business to tell them what they should do. That was a decision only they could make, and I could understand it would not be easy. On the one hand, they wanted so much to show their sympathy and their loyalty to their fellow workers; on the other, I thought that they did not want to hurt us, for we were a young business and had not had time to build a surplus and had always had friendly relations with them. I said that if they should decide to close our plant, we would not attempt to fill their places, as some other factories were doing, but would wait until the strike was over and then we wanted them to come back home and resume where they had left off.

My only suggestion was that they make their decision in a democratic way. Take a secret ballot, and let everybody agree to abide by the will of the majority. If the majority voted to go out, I thought it would be better if everyone went. If the majority voted to stay, the same rule should apply and everyone should stay in. I concluded by saying that our future action would be guided by their decision.

I learned a great deal from that experience. The usual thing for managements to have done in such a situation would have been to announce that anyone leaving his job need not expect ever to return, as there would be no job for him. But I did not believe that the reaction to threats by people who work with their hands would be so much different from that of people in managerial positions.

The workers voted almost unanimously not to go out. It was an encouraging victory for a policy that had gradually been maturing in my mind.

The shoe manufacturers of Milwaukee won the strike, if one may be said ever to win a war. They did not give in to the demands that were made, and the workers returned to work as their small savings became exhausted.

This union had no large funds with which to finance a strike and could not hope to win in the battle against the combined resources of the manufacturers. However, the lowered production over many weeks, and the disruption of organizations, caused serious losses to capital as well as labor. Many workers did not return to the factories against which they had struck. Too much bitterness had been generated for that. A worker under such circumstances usually prefers, even at a sacrifice, to make a new start in another factory. The result was a loss by both employees and the factory they left. The foremen had to break in new employees; the workers had to learn new jobs.

I thought of all the waste in money and the bitterness and humiliation of those who were forced through necessity to return to work, as well as the hostility of employers and their supervisors toward the defeated strikers; of the enmity and hatred aroused among the workers themselves, caused by some workers being more reluctant than others to strike in the first place, and by some being more eager to return to work.

How could we possibly prevent such a catastrophe in our fast-growing organization? What was it, I asked myself, that caused men to become so bitter, so vindictive, so filled with animosity that, poor as they were, they would voluntarily remove themselves from an employer's payroll and go without income for weeks and weeks in an effort to enforce their demands? We did not want our people to feel like one worker who was heard to say, "They say you gotta cooperate. You don't *gotta* do nothing 'cept die!"

Why was it necessary for workers always to accompany their demands for increased wages or for better working conditions with threats of a strike? Could it be that workers had learned that requests for increases in pay—unless accompanied by threats and with sufficient force to back up the threats—were futile? Was the real trouble, after all, dissatisfaction with wages, or was it frustration over difficulties of communication, distrust, and general misunderstanding? Might it not be possible that the worker was in the same frame of mind as an angry man whose only desire is to hurt the object of his displeasure, without any regard for the consequences?

It was not difficult to understand why the employer with such great economic strength could say with confidence to the worker, "You do as I say or get out." It was equally easy to understand why the workers after such experiences would say to the employer, when they were strong enough, "You do as we say or we will close your plant." What could we do to insure our organization against such an unhappy situation?

Was it man's inherent dislike of authority that made the trouble? Obviously, an organization could not function without authority. How could a foreman get his work done if he did not have authority to direct, to discipline, and to discharge if the situation warranted such an extreme measure? We were now dependent on foremen. We had several hundred men and women in our employ, and new ones were being added rapidly as our efforts were beginning to bear fruit.

I was perplexed by the customary prerogatives of foremen in open shops, such as the arbitrary power to hire and fire without regard to the feelings of the workers involved. The prerogative of management to fix wage rates, hours of work, and holidays (vacations and holidays with pay were unknown in those days) also disturbed me.

My thoughts went back to Hickory Street and the authoritarian attitude of the foremen under Harsh (my predecessor as superintendent). I could see that we were going to be increasingly dependent on intermediaries in the factory as my added responsibilities as co-owner of the business required more of my attention to external problems. Could we trust these men, well trained in the art of shoemaking but untrained in the attitude we were urging them to adopt? The cooperation and mutual respect established in the three and one-half years since we started was too valuable an asset to risk losing. How could our principles of justice, toleration, and understanding be preserved?

Many times we had wondered what we could do if workers came to us with demands accompanied by threats. We were positive that we would never submit to such arbitrary methods. It seemed logical to us as a consequence to assure the workers that they also would be free of arbitrary demands. The spoken or implied "Do as I say or get out" had no part in our conception of good labor relations. We had seen for too long the reaction of workers to tough methods. Arbitrary orders were obeyed only to the extent that people accepted them as fair or acquiesced through fear of disobeying.

We wondered what would happen if we should frankly say to the workers, "We will never dictate. Everything in the future must be mutually agreed upon. We will never hire a man that you don't want to work with. We will never discharge a man unless you agree he should be discharged. There will be no changes in wage rates without a discussion with you and without agreement that the new rates are fair. We will sit down with you and agree upon the days that should be observed as holidays. There will be no arbitrary edicts. Everything the management does in the future and every act will be subject to review and question. *The only authority that will be used is the authority that you have accepted.* We will agree on what is right, and both you and the management will ask the foremen to see that these things that we have agreed upon are observed. On your part, we will ask that you agree never to make any demands upon us accompanied by threats. We will outlaw threats, strikes, lockouts, and arbitrary actions of all kinds. If we ever get to the place where we can't agree on what is right, we will call in somebody from the outside who has no selfish interest in the matter and who we both feel is impartial. We will agree to abide by his decision, be it for us or against us."

We felt that management would be better off to arbitrate a matter in dispute and lose than to go through a long fight, with its inevitable cost in money and in wounded feelings on both sides that are so difficult to heal.

If the workers lost, we had faith in their willingness to take defeat in the same spirit as management. After all, defeat would not be so costly to them as a long fight, which no one ever wins. They would have had their day in court. By no stretch of the imagination would they feel as ignominious and degraded as the long-suffering striker compelled to return and seek his job from the company he has fought so unsuccessfully.

This was a revolutionary concept in the year 1915. It is even so today, but we could not see anything wrong with it. We felt that our workers would react favorably to a policy that would insure peace and encourage cooperation. No one liked to be free to do what he pleased more than I, but how could one *deny freedom from arbitrary action to another when he demanded it for himself?* How could any employer, constantly in fear of threats and sabotage, confronted with hatred, indifference, strikes, and violence, call himself free? We conceived of a new and better freedom gained through cooperation, one that would not only add to the influence of management, but also would add immeasurably to the workers' self-respect, dignity, and social status. We could not see where we were giving up anything. The industrial managers who value the prerogative of deciding everything themselves can never accomplish their purpose except as they have the power to enforce their edicts. The time always comes in the natural course of the economic cycle when workers gain the strength in turn to enforce their will.

We could see that many people would look upon such an arrangement as giving the workers control. But we knew that workers would never want to assume the heavy responsibilities of management. Participating in the making of laws is different from only accepting the responsibility of complying with them. Our ideas of democracy certainly did not visualize workers being less obedient to rules and regulations that they had participated in making. Indeed, we were sure the results would be just the opposite.

I sat down with Bush one day to find out his reaction. Bush had the natural talent of an expert counselor; he was a good listener. I had gone to him many times to discuss what seemed to me a brilliant idea, but which turned out to be a dud when subjected to the test of explanation and analysis; and sometimes without Bush saying a word.

While he had never questioned my authority in the factory, as I had never questioned his in the sales department, this was such a revolutionary thing that I felt the need of his support before going any further. Bush was a cautious man. He was anything but a pioneer. He always liked to see somebody else try out a new thing and demonstrate its soundness before taking it up himself. On the other hand, he had confidence in me, and after a thorough discussion, his advice was that I should think it over a few days longer to be sure I was right.

I have a cautious streak myself, and we finally decided that we would do a little experimenting. We would ask first only those who had served the company for three years or more to organize into a society of long-service employees. We would give these new privileges only to them. These senior employees were the men and women whom we had brought into the organization in the first six months we were in business, and of course the ones we knew the best.

So we invited all the three-year employees to the factory one evening and explained our ideas. Workers are not apt to be articulate, and particularly so in a group, but we believed in their fundamental reasonableness, and such was the case on this occasion. They were much interested in our ideas, and they readily accepted the invitation to organize into what we all agreed we would call the Nunn-Bush Cooperative Association.* The membership would include every member of the organization, regardless of his status, if he had at least three years of service.

There was no written constitution, no written agreement of any kind. The only difficulty that we could foresee was with some of the foremen, who could not help doubting whether such a plan would work. These men were all experienced shoemakers and had little experience with the kind of

---

* The name was subsequently changed to the Nunn-Bush Shop Union in 1932 and the Industrial Union of Master Craftsmen in 1934.

attitude that we were attempting to establish in the organization. I suspected that they were accepting the new plan
with unspoken reservations.

Nevertheless, no one could misunderstand the agreement,
and from that day no arbitrary action was ever taken that
affected the status of members of the association. The group
elected a business agent, who was a bench worker. We
agreed with the officers of the association that he would
be given time to perform his duties.

After a short time, the new system became so ingrained
into the attitudes of all men in authority that there was really
no difference between the way members of the association
and non-members were treated. Therefore, after one year of
experience with this new relationship, the management and
the officers of the association agreed to extend the membership and take in all two-year employees. This added to the
number in the association considerably, but the results were
the same. In fact, they were so good that in another year, the
plan was extended to cover one-year employees. Every step
we took confirmed the opinion we had formed. The more the
worker could participate in the decisions that affected his
welfare, the more he respected them and the higher regard
he had for their validity.

In May 1918 I was called to Washington to serve in the
Shoe and Leather Division of the Quartermaster's Department of the Army. I was absent from the factory for about
six months and wondered how the organization would get
along without me. Accustomed to take the lead in all con-
troversial labor matters that came up and required adjustment, I feared the consequences when I was not there.

Many people had said that the success of the system depended on my personality, and that without me it would

fail. This was not true. The organization functioned as well during my absence as it did when I was there.

With this evidence of the soundness of the principles we had adopted, I conferred with the officers of the association one day after my return and suggested that we take still another step—and a complete one—that of extending this principle of democracy to the entire shop, making everybody eligible after a 30-day probationary period. The management would employ whom they pleased and would have the right to reject such a person within 30 days if they decided during this time that he was not going to be satisfactory. The workers also would have the right to refuse him membership in the association, in which case the management would have to let the worker go. If the management did not discharge the new employee within 30 days and the association gave him a membership, he then would become a full-fledged member of the organization and have all its rights and privileges.

Up to this time, the operation of the association had involved little expense, and consequently there were no dues. The agreement between us had remained an informal, verbal understanding. No formal agreement had seemed necessary. Now, however, the committee appointed by the association to investigate my proposal to make it a 100 percent association shop decided that the members wanted a full-time business agent, to be selected either from within the organization or from without; also, a health and death benefit plan. They proposed that the expense thus incurred be shared jointly by the company and association at the ratio of two-thirds by the association and one-third by the company.

As a result of the deliberation of officers of the association and myself, representing management, we called in Dr.

Stewart Scrimshaw, of Marquette University, a man well known in the labor field and an expert in management-labor relations. We asked his help in drawing up the provisions of a formal constitution and by-laws, which the company and the association would later examine and, we hoped, would approve.

The Nunn-Bush Cooperative Association was financed jointly at first and later entirely by the workers themselves. The association had a full-time business agent who could be chosen by the workers from the outside, and could be a professional labor leader, if the workers so desired. Not only that, but the association's constitution stipulated that all managerial prerogatives of arbitrary action would be renounced. This was an entirely different conception from company unions. This was a bona fide association between capital and labor. It was an acknowledgment on management's part that labor was as important to the enterprise as was capital; it was an agreement that labor had as much right to say what they would work for as management had to say what they would pay; that labor had as much right to say with whom they would work as management had to employ whom they pleased. It was a mutual understanding that management did not have authority arbitrarily to separate a man from the payroll.

Even before the revised organization had begun to function, the management was observing principles of democracy far beyond the requirements and agreements that were in effect with the workers in union shops. Our workers had grievances, of course. Wherever large groups of workers are engaged with varying schedules and ever-changing situations requiring constant adjustment, grievances are bound to arise. In the early days, there were some workers with grievances who did not belong to the association. It made no difference; the procedure gradually began to be the same. The time soon arrived when the management would never inquire who were association members and who were not.

The grievance committee was an elected body of workers, one from each department. All grievances or suggestions were first carried to the committee, usually by the business agent, for discussion and decision. If the committee's decision was not accepted by management or by a complaining worker, it could be carried to the joint council. This board consisted of eight members: four appointed by the grievance committee and four by the management. The business agent was also privileged to attend meetings with a voice but no vote. The council's decision was final and binding on all parties. If the council's deliberation resulted in a deadlock, it was compulsory for both parties to accept arbitration.

Most of the workers' troubles never reached either the grievance committee or the joint council. When disputes developed that the foreman could not settle, often they would be brought to me. The workers would be asked to appoint a delegation to discuss the matter, and it would be considered from only one standpoint—what was right. Before we started the discussion I would be careful *first to remind myself that these workers had as much right to their opinions as I had to mine.* Then the delegation would be asked to state their case, after which I would reply in somewhat this manner: "In the first place, fellows, you should know that we frankly recognize you have as much right as the management to judge the fairness of this problem, and here is what we have to suggest. You surely will agree with me it is just. Let us get all the facts from both sides, then sit down together and consider them later today—not tomorrow. Let's see, after we get these facts, if we cannot agree on what is fair. Will you go along with me on that?"

Workers could not reject such a reasonable approach. They would go back to the department and we would begin to gather the facts on management's side, which generally could be supplied by the foreman, who, also, was usually involved in the controversy. Later in the day, at our next meeting, I was careful first to make it plain that, while I might have a suggestion to make about what we should do, it would represent only my opinion. If it did not appeal to them as fair, they were not obliged to accept it. If the facts warranted our making a concession, I tried to do it graciously and suggested that they should do the same when the shoe was on the other foot. But we always came to an agreement, and we always managed to do it without offending the other's sense of fair play. Our company and its workers never had to resort to arbitration. This would seem to be proof that when fear is removed from the human heart, reason enters. When a man is angry, he will not reason.

We always noticed that when we made a concession, it was a credit that at some later time would be repaid. Concessions beget concessions, and trust begets trust.

Our experience in finding ways to reach agreement led us more and more to abandon the practice of writing letters or posting notices on bulletin boards in the factory. When we had problems of a kind that needed to be discussed with all of the workers, rather than with a committee, I would go into each department, have the motors shut off, get on a box, have the people gather around me, and discuss the matter informally, just as I did at the time of the shoe industry strike in Milwaukee in 1914. We found this effective. I asked for cooperation, and cooperation soon became the watchword of the organization. We constantly urged the workers to call our attention to anything the company did that they did not consider just or that they felt should be done differently. We wanted to impress everyone with the idea that no one, from the head of the business to the humblest worker, was so good or so smart or so important that he could afford to be arbitrary. Every question, every rule, every order was open to question, discussion, and decision—decision not by any one individual, but by the majority.

The new constitution and by-laws of the association gave the company's attorneys quite a shock. They were much disturbed over the provisions as agreed upon by the workers' committee and myself after consultation with Dr. Scrimshaw. Before preparing the papers they sent for Bush and Weldon, my associates, and asked them if they really understood what the factory management was doing. They explained to them that, if the company accepted the association constitution, the prerogatives of arbitrary decisions would be taken away from the board of directors, and they did not believe that it should be done. They went on to say that under the law only the directors had authority to run the business. Management's right to discharge employees was a prerogative that could not be surrendered. It was unrealistic for anyone to think that discipline in a large organization could be maintained without this authority, and they urged my associates to set me straight.

Bush and Weldon came to me much disturbed, and, while they still had faith in my judgment, they asked if I really understood how serious and revolutionary these proposals were.

"Well, we have been working this way for four years," I said to them. "We are not proposing to do anything new. We are only putting verbal agreements into written form, and, as you know, these agreements have made for satisfactory relations with our workers. On the other hand, these lawyers' other clients have been continually having strikes and labor troubles. It's true their managements have not renounced any prerogatives, but neither have they secured the good will of the workers, and they have not been able to enforce their demands. It is all right for management to have the right to demand certain things, but having the right to demand and getting it are two entirely different things."

I asked them frankly if they did not think my influence with the workers in the factory was more effective in getting cooperation than all the power we had renounced. They were inclined to agree and, after asking me to give the matter further thought before requesting the board to approve the new constitution and by-laws of the association, they left the matter in my hands. It required little further consideration, and in a few days I sent the new constitution and by-laws to the board for their approval, which was immediately granted. The more I considered the principles involved, the more convinced I was that we were on the right track.

I thought of the chief characteristics of our political democracy—freedom of speech; the individual's right to oppose the majority, and, at the same time, his duty to abide by majority rule after it had been declared. I pondered on the fact that in our political democracy even the chief executive's power is limited. He is responsible to his constituents; and even the veto of the President of the United States can be overriden by a two-third's vote of the Congress. I recalled how all our laws were made by representatives elected by the people, and how the executive could only sign or veto these laws, but not initiate them. Finally, and above everything else, I thought of the *supremacy of law* in our political democracy, with all differences being settled by judicial process; I thought of the right of the individual to be tried by his peers. These principles had been thoroughly tested, and I could see no reason why they were not in the main as applicable to industrial organization as they were to governments.

In the workshops of the world, as business functions today, so-called managerial prerogatives provide for those in authority to impose their will in varying degrees on those below at every level of management. The executive in industry is not responsible to the workers. Top management usually makes policy without consulting the workers, and primarily with only the interests of stockholders in mind.

Freedom of speech by workers is seldom practiced without peril of separation from the payroll; the grievance of a disgruntled worker has little chance of getting beyond his immediate supervisor in shops with no labor unions or organized machinery for such matters.

We became so enthusiastic about the principle of participation by labor that, in agreement with the workers, we placed signs in all departments, principally for the benefit of the newer employees. They read as follows:

DEMOCRACY

In this factory all rules are made *jointly* by management and workers.

No individual has to do as some other individual dictates.

We all do as we all agree we all should do.

Some of the liberal ideas of Woodrow Wilson, who was President during these formative years of the association, had much influence on our thinking. I particularly liked something he said at the end of World War I:

There must be a genuine democratization of industry based upon a full recognition of the right of those who work, in whatever rank, to participate in some organic way in every decision which directly affects their welfare, or the part they are to play in industry.

There have been only two occasions when we came even close to calling in an arbitrator.

The first instance came during the severe depression that began in 1930. The management had made a change in the system of conveying shoes, changing from a 24-pair to a 12-pair rack. The edge trimmers* brought up a grievance, claiming that this change was reducing their speed and asking for some adjustment in the amount of work they were to do for the pay they were receiving.

Up to this time every question that had come up to the joint council had been resolved without difficulty by the council itself. This rack problem was discussed at several meetings of the joint council. Finally, a committee was appointed to visit other factories where this change had been made to see what their experience had been. The committee reported back to the council that there had been no complaint on the part of the workers in these other plants, and, while the worker-members of the committee would not admit it, the result of the investigation on the whole was favorable to the management's viewpoint.

When the vote was taken, the result was four votes for the grievance and four votes against it. The worker representatives had stood solid for the edge-trimmers' position, and the management representatives had presented a solid front for the view of management. The worker-chairman of the joint council then announced that he presumed the disagreement would have to go to arbitration. The matter was not important, and we had such a long record of never taking anything to arbitration that I spoke up as a member of the management group and stated that I would change my vote and accept the workers' viewpoint. The chairman then said,

* A skilled operation of shaping the edge of the soles. An operator holds the shoe containing the last against fast-revolving edge-cutters made to fit the particular sole being trimmed.

"Well, that settles the argument as to whether there is a grievance. The next thing is to decide how much work should be reduced on account of this change in the racks."

At this announcement of the chairman, the business agent spoke up and said, "I am authorized by the edge-trimmers to leave the question of amount of change to Mr. Nunn."

"Well," I said, "I don't think that is fair, because you know that I don't think there is any grievance, and it doesn't seem just to the edge-trimmers to leave it to me."

"No," the business agent said, "that is what they want— you are to decide the amount."

It was hard to understand this unexpected action of the edge-trimmers. I felt that deep in their hearts they knew the management was right. We had argued the matter so much it was difficult for them, after having taken such a strong position, to withdraw. So, we made a slight adjustment in the schedule and they were satisfied. The workers had won their point, and that was the important thing to them. It was one more proof to me that the labor problem is more psychological than it is economic. We suspected the edge-trimmers were more interested in winning their battle and saving face than they were in doing less work.

It was not until years later that we realized where we had made our mistake and how easy it would have been for us to have avoided the controversy in the first place. The mistake, as we should have known, was in arbitrarily changing the racks from 24- to 12-pair without consulting the workers concerned. We took too much for granted. There were many more advantages to the 12-pair rack than there were disadvantages. If we had asked the edge-trimmers to participate in the decision about the racks, there is no question in my mind that they would have voted for the change.

By our carelessness in acting arbitrarily, we gave one man

(who, as I discovered many years later, really was dissatisfied about an entirely different matter) the opportunity of seizing on this action and enlisting the support of his fellows. While his brother workers sided with him 100 percent when he based his grievance on management's being arbitrary in installing new racks, they probably would never have agreed with him on his real grievance. The worker who initiated the complaint was really unhappy because the foreman did not think the quality of his work justified his trimming the edges of the top-grade shoes and consequently required his doing a larger number of pairs for the same wage. It is humiliating now to realize how much later it was before I discovered where I had made my mistake.

This is a good example of how costly arbitrary action can be to a company. One man out of fifteen was able to cause trouble, whereas, if we had used democratic procedures and taken a vote in the first place, a minority of even seven could not have enlisted support from the majority later.

The other case that barely escaped arbitration was the question of employment of married women. During the hard time of the 1930's, when so many people did not have employment, many workers felt that married women should not work outside the home. They believed that, when many married men and single girls were unemployed, a man and his wife should not both be holding jobs.

These workers did not stop to consider that there might be special circumstances that would require the married woman to work, and that it was a difficult task for management to have the facts necessary to judge each case fairly.

During this extreme emergency when jobs were so scarce our management did use special care to give the few jobs they had to those who needed them most. But that was a special situation. After the depression was over, the management took the position that it was not for them to judge a woman's need, but only her fitness for the job. We had no way of knowing whether the husband was able to make a living for the family. He might be physically incapacitated. Not only that, but the woman herself might prefer to hire someone to do her housework and earn money in the factory with which to pay her help. In any event, she had the same rights as a man, and, if she wanted to work, that was her business. We agreed that as a general proposition it might be better for a married woman to stay home and take care of her children and her husband, but that was a matter for her to decide, and not the management of an industry.

This matter, like the rack matter, was discussed for many weeks. The management insisted they were right, and finally said to the workers' executive board.* "This is a matter of principle, and we can't back down on it. It is something that will have to go to arbitration if we cannot persuade you that the right is on our side."

It was only then that the opposition began to weaken. Louis Ritter, the secretary and attorney for the workers, spoke up and said, "H.L., we don't want to break our record and arbitrate this matter. We believe we should be big enough to wash our dirty linen inside the shop as we always have, and I believe the members of the board will agree that we will drop the matter for the present." So, once more, we

---

* Formerly called the grievance committee. This was one of the changes required by the Wagner National Labor Relations Act in 1935. These changes were merely technical and did not affect our fundamental relationship. As required by the Act, all persons of authority in the company withdrew from the workers' organization. The joint council was changed from a formal to an informal committee. When the executive board had grievances or suggestions to bring up, they would appoint a subcommittee to meet with members of management. The contract beween the new union and the company had the same provisions in it as had been in the old association by-laws: No one was to be arbitrary; if the management and the workers could not agree, they were to arbitrate.

avoided arbitration. This time it was a victory for the management, and the matter has never come up again.

Another matter that came up during the Second World War in this same factory illustrates once more the willingness of people to support decisions in which they have participated.

It has always been a problem of management to control smoking within a factory. It is a fire hazard and extremely dangerous to life in factories where inflammable materials are used and the building has many occupants. Where people are working with their hands, it is usually considered a hindrance to efficient work. In all factories of this nature, strict rules are made against it. The rules are usually broken in varying degrees, and there is a certain amount of smoking in secluded areas, such as rest rooms, back stairs, and fire escapes.

In some factory offices, everyone is permitted to smoke; in others, only the male employees; in still others, only the officers and high executives enjoying the seclusion of a private office.

In our case, the rule had originally been made against smoking in the factory before the association was ever formed, and it was only fairly well observed. No serious attempt was made to tighten enforcement until wartime sabotage became a matter of concern. It was at the start of the Second World War that the executive board of the union, together with management, appointed a joint safety committee to make an inspection and report.

Inasmuch as I had detected an occasional violation of the rule in the factory, such as an impatient smoker sometimes lighting up his cigarette while on the stairway going out in the evening, I was delighted to hear of the project. I was a smoker myself, but willing to sacrifice the habit while in my

office or the factory, if by doing so it would aid in the effort
to reduce fire hazard in the factory and help the cause of
efficiency.

I readily agreed that the rule might be observed more
faithfully if we would include the general and administrative offices. I could understand why a worker might feel like
ignoring a rule when he could see that it did not apply to
everyone alike. Why should we officers take privileges denied to others?

The recommendation to prohibit smoking in all parts of
the factory and offices, excepting only the recreation hall and
dining room, was made and accepted by both the executive
board of the union and the management. The rule has been
in effect since 1942, and for all these years it has been strictly
observed. Arbitrary edicts by management have never produced a like result.

Of all the recognized prerogatives of management, none
occupies such a hallowed position as the right to choose, in-
dependently and without consultation, those men in each
echelon of the managerial chain of command to be given
authority to direct others. However, it is recognized today by
good managements that a supervisor should not only have
knowledge of the work he is to supervise and the ability to
inspire employees to want to do the work, but also the capacity to bring out the workers' potential. In order to accomplish this purpose, administrators with a good knowledge of human relations recognize that the man appointed
must be acceptable to the workers whom he is to direct.

We had a vacancy in one of our departments and Jack
LeRoach, a machine worker in the same department, was
recommended by the retiring foreman as a good man to succeed him. I knew little about Jack, except that he had been
with us for some time and was a good worker. We had con-

fidence, however, in the foreman's judgment and, carrying out our policy of making promotions from within the plant, announced that Jack would be appointed. Shortly after this announcement was made, the retiring foreman came to my office with a worried look and said, "H.L., I'm in trouble. Some of the men in the room don't like Jack, and they are showing their dislike by not getting the work out. What shall I do?"

Obviously, a mistake had been made. In talking with some of the old-timers in the department, I was told that Jack had been one of those individuals who had not gone along with the group. Some of the things that made him popular with the foreman had made him unpopular with the rest of the men in the department. Without hesitation, I called Jack into my office and told him frankly that we had moved too fast; that he could never make a success under the circumstances; that the management thought well of him; and that the day would come no doubt, when he could be given a supervisory job, but we would have to make a new start.

After consultation with the business agent of the union, we decided on another man and had the business agent talk with some of the leaders to find out if he were acceptable. Upon receiving a good report, he was appointed. We had no further trouble.

Jack LeRoach was sent to another department to make a new start. He later became foreman and later still was promoted to foreman of one of the most important departments in the factory, but only after I had consulted the business agent of the union and learned that LeRoach would be given the support of those he had been chosen to lead.

As an illustration of how little a manager really knows of what may be going on in his factory, I should say that eight years after I retired from the factory I was informed by one of the participants in this episode that the workers' dislike of Jack LeRoach was really not for the reason given at the time but because he had been the cause of a popular fellow-worker's broken home.

After this experience we never again appointed a supervisor without first consulting the business agent and through him sounding out the sentiment of the room. In some cases I talked directly with certain old employees in the room and, after securing their agreement that the man proposed would be acceptable, I would ask and receive their promise to give him their support in making a success of the job. Workers appreciate this kind of consideration by management.

This was only a partial step in workers' participation in the selection of the man who is to direct their work. However, as far as this particular organization was concerned, it seemed to be as far as the workers themselves wanted to go. If I were managing this plant today and I found that the workers wished to go further in the selection of someone to direct them, I would acquiesce. At the same time, let me quickly emphasize that I recognize that this kind of system might not work in every factory. Factories that have neither background of participation and democratic administration nor understanding of economic mutuality of interests, would conceivably run into trouble.

Under the Nunn-Bush Plan, the responsibility of management to manage the business is in no way lessened or in any way usurped by labor. Only the method of managing has been changed. With customary arbitrary prerogatives surrendered, management now rules under democratic rather than autocratic principles.

Recognition of workers' right to a fair share of production means that management ceases buying labor as one would buy coal or any other commodity. A mature and realistic relationship has added dignity, respect, and faith in a common as well as a free enterprise.

Operating under democratic principles produces these results:

1. Workers have their solidarity, and each worker is free to oppose the majority until the vote is taken, after which he democratically accepts the decision.
2. Management's power is limited and every act is subject to question and acceptance.
3. Policy is made by management after consultation with representatives of labor and consideration of the workers' interest as well as those of the stockholders.
4. Everyone enjoys freedom of speech and all communication.
5. Law is supreme, with differences settled not by force on either side but by judicial or semijudicial processes.

7

THE LOT OF THE WORKER

"A working man can never have any money anyway." This was the statement of Art Strege, an outspoken "puller-over" in our lasting room, at a joint council meeting many years ago. Art's words came as quite a shock, and I listened intently as he continued. "It takes every cent a guy can make to meet his needs when he works, and if he does not get full time he is sure to get behind. Every day when I walk to work I wonder if we will have full time next week. The little apartment I live in is as small and cheap as I can get. I don't know how fellows with bigger families than mine make out at all. It wouldn't be so bad if we could only know we would get a full check every week, but as it is, it's kind of hopeless, and you don't care whether you save a dollar or two some weeks or not. If you do, they are soon gone when a lay-off comes. So, what's the difference? You get so you don't care—money don't mean much—you can't keep it very long anyway."

Art Strege had always been a good and dependable worker, and I turned to him and said, "What do you mean, Art, by saying that money does not mean much to a working man?"

"Just this," Art replied. "Mighty few working people are

ever caught up on their debts. When they get their pay-checks, they pay their rent, their grocery bill, and maybe make a payment on their furniture and doctor bill. There is damned little left, if anything. Some weeks I hardly have enough for cigarette money. You get discouraged. Of course, I suppose everyone wants more money, but it doesn't seem to help when you get it—your rent goes up—your grocery bills too. Whatever happens, you stay broke, so what the hell!"

While I was surprised at Art's pessimism, I did not resent what he said. After the meeting I talked to Louis Karl, the business agent of the association, and asked him to tell me frankly what he thought about what Art had said. Louis replied, "Well, H. L., Art is not feeling good today and must be sore about something, but really you can't blame him for feeling that the worker does get the dirty end of the stick. It is sort of a hopeless outlook. He has to get his satisfaction out of life in a different way, and I don't think he should. I sometimes wonder myself if some men are entitled to so much when the workers who sweat and toil to produce the money get so little. Now, don't get me wrong; I don't mean to say that managers should not make many times what the worker does. But I sometimes wonder if God in heaven, looking down upon the earth, sees men digging ditches and mining coal and drilling for oil and working the farms and in the factories, and many of them living as they have to live. If God sees all this, what does He think about it? It wouldn't be quite so bad, H. L., if the worker could only know how much he could hope to make for the year so he could make a budget and plan his life as salaried people can do."

Although this incident took place nearly forty years ago, I recall that even then I sensed with deep concern that if there was something in our economic system that created such social and psychological attitudes, these attitudes in turn could not help but have harmful results on economic efficiency. Today, as I reflect on my experience of a lifetime in working with men and women in industry, I consider this relationship between economic factors and social and psychological factors to be the most fundamental of all the causes involved in our battle to win for the capitalistic system the ideological struggle with communism.

The Restriction of the Wage Earner to a Bare "Living Wage"

It was only after my own economic security became more assured that I came to a real awareness of the insecure position of the manual worker as industry is organized today. Although the words of Art Strege and Louis Karl had continued to live in my memory, it took many years before I began to understand the true reasons why it should seem to these men that the worker is limited by our economic system to at best a bare "living wage" that provides scant opportunity to save and accumulate. What is more, I have come to conclude that as our economic system operates today, Art and Louis are not far from right. Despite the fact that hourly wage earners are not as poor today, thanks to the progress of technology and the efforts of organized labor, as practically all were forty years ago, even today 8 percent of all families in the United States are living on a total income of $1,000 or less, and nearly one-third on less than $3,000.*

It must be remembered that, as industry has become increasingly large in size, the organization has grown in importance and overshadowed the individual, whose personal feelings, emotions, and ambitions are further and further removed from those who are best qualified to judge him. The

* *Federal Reserve Bank Bulletin*, September, 1958.

gonius, who advanced to a top position so fast when businesses were small, is now increasingly in danger of never having his talents discovered.

The great mass of laboring people cannot hope to rise from their status as workers to that of managerial or professional rank, nor can they have much hope of becoming entrepreneurs under our ever-growing tendency to increase the production of both agricultural and factory products through mass means and huge organizations. The worker is far more class-bound than he was in the early days of our economic growth.

I am not unaware that many men have risen from the ranks of labor and obscurity to great affluence. This kind of opportunity has been one of the advantages of a free-enterprise system and, consequently, has made the system very dear to those who have been able, by talent, enterprise, and good luck, to take advantage of such opportunities. But the percentage of men without special talent and without compelling ambition and without luck—and luck is a real factor, as I have good reason to know—is very large. The overwhelming majority of workers fall into these categories. It is only for those few fortunates who manage to leave the ranks of manual workers that there is hope for more than the uncertain struggle to eke out a bare living wage. For the many who remain, our economic system today does limit the opportunities for economic gain, no matter how well the commodity they produce is made.

This is not true for the man who *sells* the product that the manual workers produce. Usually there is no ceiling to *his* potential compensation. There are travelling salesmen who earn $25,000, $50,000, $60,000 per year and even more—perhaps six to twelve times more than the skilled men who make the product. It is axiomatic that the better the product, the easier it is to sell, and the more efficiently made, the lower the price and, again, the easier to sell. It would be possible to argue that the factors that often make the product so desirable and add so quickly to the salesman's income are often factors for which the workers, rather than the seller, should be rewarded.

Limitation on the income of the worker is not a misconception in the minds of the men who, like Art and Louis, struggle to meet their daily bills, nor does it come about by chance. It is a direct by-product of the fallacious but prevailing idea that dominates our economic views today—that the labor of the working man is a commodity to be bought and sold according to supply and demand. This is the concept adhered to both by management, which tries to buy at the lowest available price, and by labor, which tries to sell at the highest possible figure. This is the concept that places, in the long run, the rigid limitation upon the compensation of labor at a little more than the bare subsistence level of a "living wage." This is the concept that the Nunn-Bush Plan, described in Part One of this book, completely rejects in favor of a concept of partners in production.

As long as our economy persists in the view that the manual worker is as interchangeable a part of the production process as is some machine or some part of a machine, there is little likelihood of turning toward some better way for the compensation of labor, such as that built into the Nunn-Bush Share-Production Plan. After all, there is no necessary or logical reason for providing a machine with more power or lubrication than its operation requires. Why then should management feel concern for reimbursing the working man beyond the level required for subsistence and good health? I grant, of course, that many good men of management, moved by humanitarian motives, have felt this concern and acted upon it. However, I maintain that, despite exceptions, the concept of labor as a commodity does pre dominate in our economic system, and it does operate to put a limit on the earning potential of the working man.

The Economic Consequences of Social and Psychological Factors

Just as the economic conditions that result from this unfortunate economic concept produce unfortunate social and psychological attitudes in the minds of working men, so in turn *their* social and psychological attitudes eventually lead to further unfortunate economic conditions.

The great fallacy of the commodity concept of labor is that it tempts men of management to minimize this psychological factor and sometimes misleads them into ignoring it entirely.

Often I have heard spokesmen for capital make such statements as, "It takes $10,000 to give a man a job." Inasmuch as the *man* creates the wealth with his labor, and inasmuch as property would have no value except as made productive through the brain, skill, and labor of man, we should say with more accuracy, "It takes a man to give $10,000 a job." In the Middle Ages, after the dissolution of feudal relationships and the rise of the guild system, the concept of property being used for man, rather than man for property, was an ethical standard accepted by Church and society in general. Only with the industrial revolution came the concept of labor as a commodity to be bought and sold, and the consequent reversal of values.

If we are to understand our industrial system and are to take the steps necessary to cure the ills that plague it, we can do so only if we first understand the full implications of this reversal of values. If, ostrich-like, blinded by this idea that labor is a commodity, we persist in ignoring the importance of social and psychological values to economic success, all our best-intentioned efforts to cure the weaknesses of capitalism will be futile. Only through a clear recognition of this importance can we find the path to the major changes that alone hold promises of success.

I do not subscribe to the notion that men of management and capital do not desire to improve the lot of the working man. It is not lack of good intentions that stands in the way, it is the false idea so many men of management have of labor's rightful place in industry. It has been the tendency of these business leaders to view the worker as an irresponsible, unwilling, and reluctant tool to be used for the achievement of their ambitions; it has been the failure of these men to understand how their own social and psychological attitudes affect the attitude of the worker that has been at fault. Only when men of both capital and labor abandon the concept of labor as a commodity to be bought and sold will they begin diligently searching for new ways to give this essential element of industrial enterprise the status and position of dignity its importance demands. Only then will the way to industrial peace and prosperity be found.

Arbitrary Power in the Open Shop

Probably no other one thing does as much to create insecure and hostile psychological attitudes in working men as the misuse of arbitrary power. Man's instinctive will to power seems to be little different from that of primitive society. The will to live, to succeed, to be recognized, to be important, to exploit the weak—these are natural instincts that society has been able to control only through processes of law. In few walks of life in civilized society has the right to arbitrary power been so little challenged as in our industrial enterprises. Bolstered by the general unquestioned acceptance of the commodity concept of labor, the abuse of arbitrary power has wrought untold damage to the social and psychological attitudes of workers. Many instances of the misuse of power in an open shop that I have observed serve to impress this point in my memory.

For example, while working in the capacity of cashier in a large midwestern shoe factory in the spring of 1904, I received from the hands of a worker an order signed by his foreman to pay him in full all wages due, as he was being discharged for "staying out without permission one Saturday afternoon last January."

The foreman in this shop hired and fired all the help without consulting the superintendent or anybody else. He had absolute authority, and he used it in varying degrees. The worker involved seemed so despondent as I paid him the balance of wages due that it excited my interest, and I took the first opportunity to ask the foreman who discharged him about the circumstances. It seems that this man had some months previously asked for permission to stay out one Saturday afternoon. Permission was denied, but the man must have had some compelling need—for jobs were not easy to get, and he must have known the risk involved—because he disregarded the foreman's orders and stayed out anyway. The foreman, not able to replace him on Monday morning, said to himself, "O.K., old man, I'll let you go back to work today, but when I can locate a man to take your place, out you go."

Even though months had passed, this foreman saw no injustice in making the replacement at *his* convenience, rather than immediately after the offense was committed. To me, it seemed brutal. I grant that some punishment was due. Dismissal, while severe, might be justified by a strict disciplinarian. But to wait for months and then to dismiss without any notice and without any regard for the necessities of the worker could not be justified by any code of right conduct. What must have been the reaction of this man's fellow workers? Certainly it was not admiration or respect for their foreman. He could only have aroused their hatred mixed with fear. Apparently this foreman had never thought of the possibility of ruling other men except through fear of the power he held.

I remember another occasion when I received a discharge slip with reason for discharge given as "Dissatisfied." I knew the man being discharged. He had been with us longer than the foreman who discharged him, and to me had always seemed an excellent employee. Later, when I asked the foreman about the circumstances connected with his action, he said: "This man asked me for a raise in pay and I told him I would look up the records and let him know later. After the dismissal bell at 6 P.M. I purposely asked him to wait at my desk, because I did not want him to contact the other men. After the others were gone, I made out his discharge slip and told him to get his money because he was through."

This man had told me himself that he did not want to lose his job, and he had told the foreman that he would stay for his present wage, but the foreman had replied: "No, I don't want you to stay because you are dissatisfied, and if you stay you will make the others dissatisfied."

It is with deep shame that I vividly recall an incident that occurred in the Cape Girardeau factory in the early days of its organization.

Returning from lunch one day, I found a "round robin"* on my desk, signed by all the workers in the lasting room, demanding an increase in pay. These men were all inexperienced workers, hired several months before, and were paid $3.50 per week while learning. They were privileged to go on piece work as soon as they could do enough work to earn more than their starting rate. I had estimated, on the basis of my knowledge of how much work an experienced man could do, that they would be able to earn a maximum of about $13.50 per week, compared with $18.00 they could probably earn in the city of St. Louis.

After looking over the names on this "round robin," I picked out one of the lasters by the name of Jim Redfield—a man I knew well and suspected of being a leader of the group—and sent for him to come to my office. After telling him sharply that I was disappointed with his action and that of his fellow workers, I explained to him how the company had started this factory so that work could be provided for the unemployed, and how expensive it was to teach so many people at one time the art of shoemaking. Now that these men were beginning to earn more than the starting rate, it seemed ungrateful of them to make such demands.

Jim disclaimed leadership and said he had only signed the "round robin" because everyone else was doing so. He was willing to continue on the job without change of conditions, and would do so. He would also do everything he could to satisfy the others. "Jim," I said, "if you are sure you feel that way, I want you to sign a statement I will prepare. Otherwise I am going to send for your coat and hat, pay you up to date, and you can go on your way. I do not want you to return to the department unless you are sure you are

* A demand by workers, in circular form in order to disguise the order of signing.

satisfied with our conditions." Jim replied that he did not want to lose his job and would sign anything that I prepared. I then wrote a statement to the effect that he was satisfied, would return to work, and would do what he could to satisfy the others. It stated furthermore that if he violated this agreement, he would default any pay that might be due him.

Arbitrary Power in the Union Shop

It is true that if this situation had come up in St. Louis, Jim Redfield and his shopmates might not have been so servile. In Cape Girardeau there were few opportunities for steady industrial work other than the shoe factory. In St. Louis, organization of labor was a constant threat; in Cape Girardeau, my power had no such deterrent.

The rise of organized labor did not bring an end to unilateral action. Despite the progress by unions in collective bargaining in such matters as wage rates, vacations with pay, sick leave, holidays, overtime rates, insurance, pensions, and what not, the fact is that even in the union shop today the worker often finds himself alone and absolutely dependent on the fairness of one man who, in turn, is dependent on just one thing in order to insure *himself* of economic progress— his ability to get the work done at the least possible cost. As a general rule, a worker who attempts to go higher than his immediate supervisor will instantly be referred to the man who is directly responsible for his conduct.

Although the dictatorial practices of my Hickory Street and Cape Girardeau days no longer exist in the same brutal form, the same managerial prerogatives are recognized and the same ends are often accomplished today by subtler means. Indeed, organized labor in general, rather than challenging the right to the existence of such power, has pre-

ferred to accept it by meeting the arbitrary power of management whenever possible with equal arbitrary power of
its own.

Managerial Ethics

In a public discussion some months ago on the subject of
managerial ethics, one of my fellow panel members stated
that everyone in his organization had a boss. "True enough,"
was my reply, "but not everyone in an organization such as
yours has someone he can boss." To give orders with increasing assurance as one climbs the ladder of success in an authoritarian organization may warm the cockles of one's
heart, but those who are compelled always to listen, but to
whom no one in authority, in turn, will ever pay the least attention, are condemned to an existence that surely dulls the
independent thinking processes.

In failing to sense this difference, my fellow panelist was
demonstrating an all-too-common lack of sensitivity to important psychological factors. A more complete understanding would make it impossible to defend, from any ethical
standpoint, certain managerial practices now in common use.

For example, I have long been concerned about the matter
of references from former employers. Too often, the worker
suffers from the mistakes of former employers, rather than
his own. He may have been misplaced—capable in some
kind of work that he had no chance to try, but most incapable in the work assigned. He may have had frustrations
at home or in the shop during the period of his employment,
unknown to those who make it their business to assess his
worth and report to an inquiring employer. An illness may
have temporarily decreased his efficiency. An incompetent

supervisor may have been more the cause of his failure than any lack of ability on his part.

When a man who must have work is deprived of the chance to get it through some misplaced sense of loyalty or cooperation between one employer and another, I feel cause for serious concern. There are so many possible explanations for failure or even for behavior in violation of factory rules deserving of discharge, that it is presumptuous for any man to deny a worker some future opportunity. The little good that may be claimed for such a practice is negligible when weighed against the irreparable harm that may be done by such blatant lack of concern for human values.

There is another practice even worse, based on a code of ethics that clearly puts dollars before men: the custom of refusing employment to those already employed. I became aware of this practice some 50 years ago, when in one large city in which I was working the shoe manufacturing association kept a file of employees of its members. A shoe factory could not put a man or woman to work without receiving information from this source that the applicant had severed his connection with a former employer for a period of at least three days. If a worker wanted to better himself, he was obliged to resign his job and take the great risk of securing another.

I discovered that this inhuman system is more deeply entrenched in Europe than here. On a mission for the Economic Cooperation Administration (Marshall Plan) of our government in the summer of 1951, a small group of business and professional men of which I was the leader had occasion to visit many factories in France, Holland, and Germany. I was distressed to learn that in these countries employers admitted openly the practice of not employing each other's employees. Statement to this effect would be freely made with the apparent conviction that such a practice was a natural and recognized prerogative of management. I was stunned at the time, because I had an idea that this custom so prevalent years ago, was not now in common use. Such is not the case. Even today, as these words are written, many employment departments in the United States are reluctant to offer positions to applicants presently employed by a competitor. The worker should not be compelled to take the unemployment risk involved in leaving a less desirable job in order to seek a better one. In some communities where jobs are scarce such a practice has many aspects of slavery, in that a worker is given no opportunity to put his services on the open market without a risk he cannot afford to take.

Our National Labor Relations Act points out many practices of employers as unfair, but few of the things mentioned in this Act compare in importance to the fundamental right of every human being to seek employment and to have his application considered on its merits anywhere and with any company that is in a position to use his services. To deny this right is to deny men one of the most precious rights a free people can have: the right to seek work with whom one pleases, and have one's application given consideration without regard to present employment.

Agitators and Freedom of Speech

I have been particularly impressed over the years by management's extreme dislike of what it usually chooses to call "agitators." I am not speaking of the occasional saboteur who uses his position within the organization for the purpose of tearing it down—one who may be paid to make trouble and has some ulterior motive in his obstructive tactics. Such a man, admittedly, is not amenable to reason and must be separated from the organization as soon as possible. I am concerned here with the average dissatisfied but honest employee who happens to be unusually articulate.

Too many managers seem to be unconscious of the fact that the agitator's real attitude is little, if any, different from his fellow workers. The slightest knowledge of human behavior should enable management to perceive that an hourly wage-earner's insecurity and futile position would develop thoughts not often openly expressed.

It is easy to conceive also that these thoughts might not always be flattering to management. In every large group there is usually *one* articulate and courageous individual who takes great personal satisfaction in giving expressions to such uncomplimentary thoughts, which usually arouse quick and enthusiastic approval of his fellow-workers.

The word "agitator" was much more in common use before the Wagner National Labor Relations Act was made a law in 1935. While factory workers were more frequently discharged in those days for "agitating," the so-called "troublemaker" is still with us.

I learned to understand this attitude of workers who, it seemed to me, were nothing more than brave leaders who saw no harm in striving to improve the lot of the worker through a knowledge of strength in union.

Nothing can be more frustrating to a factory worker than the fear of expressing his thoughts lest he get in trouble with his boss—and I dare say managements, in general, have given far too little consideration to the effect on morale of the common managerial attitude.

I made up my mind early in my experience as a factory manager that I would be tolerant of agitators. Having had experience with a tough superintendent and tough foremen, I could make allowances for workers' seeming intolerance.

I thought I could see that they reflected the general attitude of men ruled by authoritarian methods. They earned their reputation as agitators only because of their courage in expressing the feelings of the group.

Agitators never seem to quit their jobs. The man who does not show up for work, and never says why, is more likely to be the quiet fellow who keeps his trouble to himself and finally reaches the point where steam has to be let out. Unable to find the words or the courage to express his feelings, his only recourse, his only means of striking back, is to stay away and hope his tormentor will be hurt by not easily finding someone immediately to take his place.

Even though the present National Labor Relations Act defines the discharge of an employee for advocating collective action on the part of workers as an unfair labor practice, the worker who insists on speaking his mind—or, to use the employer's word "agitating"—is likely to find himself discharged for some other reason that *is* legal.

I was intrigued with the thought of using these qualities of courage and articulateness, possessed by only a few workers among the many, to our own advantage. Why not see if I could not sell these obstreperous fellows, and girls too, on the justice of the company's actions and the fairness of our policies? Make friends of them. Give them every consideration. By convincing them of our sincerity in conceding their right to speak their mind, we would gain their respect and, even more, their friendship. Perhaps I could learn something about the things that bothered workers—things that management usually considered of little significance. Most important of all, perhaps I could eventually influence these fellows to begin agitating *for* the company, rather than against it.

The man who keeps quiet over things he does not like will

also keep quiet when conditions are pleasing to him. Therefore, it is more important to have the outspoken employee
believing in the rightness of the company's policies and
actions than anyone else. This kind of thinking prompted me
to make it plain, a short time after we established our own
business, that workers had a right to complain *openly* and
freely when conditions did not please them—and we didn't
care if they used rough language in the process.

Our company once had an agitator who was so opinion-
ated, so unreasonable, and so impossible to satisfy that even
Walter Shenk, the business agent of the union, lost patience
with him. This agitator did not confine his attacks to the
company management; in his eyes, everything seemed to be
wrong. He apparently did not like anybody connected with
the company, including the union and its officials.

Nothing would have pleased Walter more than to have
the fellow quit his job. "Why does he stay," Walter once said
to me, "if he thinks conditions are so bad?" I could not help
feeling much as Walter did, and it was only my pride in our
policy of trying to convert agitators that enabled me to be
patient.

Without my knowledge, Walter decided to do some detective work. He was determined to find out what kind of person this fellow really was. He knew where the man usually
cashed his paycheck and he planted a friend in this tavern—
a man our agitator did not know. The friend was instructed
to get acquainted with him and sound him out on his real
feelings about the company and the union. Walter's idea was
that the agitator, not knowing the new acquaintance had any
connection with or knowledge of the company, would say
what he really thought.

When our "beefer" laid his check on the tavern bar,
Walter's amateur detective said, "I notice you work at Nunn-
Bush."

"Yes," our man replied.

"They tell me that is a helluva shop to work in."

"Oh, I wouldn't say that—what the hell do you know about it, anyway?"

"Believe me, fella, I know a lot. Guys have told me the company is rotten, the bosses slave drivers, and the union leaders company stooges—anything else you want to know?"

The Nunn-Bush worker put his glass of beer down, looked Walter's detective straight in the eye, and in a most belligerent manner spit out his words so fast and so heatedly that it was hard to understand what he was saying. The general tenor of his remarks, however, was that Walter's friend did not know what he was talking about, and that as far as he was concerned, he considered it the best damned shop he had ever worked in.

Walter, with a big smile on his face, brought the news to me. We both agreed that it was not always easy to interpret a worker's thoughts by what he said.

It was only a few years after we started our business and not long after the big strike in the large shoe factories of Milwaukee that a brother manufacturer called me on the telephone and said, "Nunn, I have just learned that you have a man named Hamilton working for you, Arthur Hamilton. He was one of the strikers in our plant and is a trouble-maker. If you will take a little friendly advice from me, you will get rid of him as quickly as you can."

At the time I really did not know who Hamilton was, and I immediately went to the foreman and made inquiry. The foreman came from the same upstate town and had known him for a long time. The foreman said that he was a good worker and, if handled right, would make a good employee.

I soon had an opportunity to talk to Art and was favorably impressed. He had one defective eye that had been so badly injured he could not see out of it—not to mention its unsightliness. Even so, there was something attractive about his face. He had a pleasing personality and impressed me as being not only articulate, but competent and sincere. My judgment was soon vindicated. Hamilton proved to be an excellent worker. He was selected by the Nunn-Bush Cooperative Association as its first business agent; he was later given a position by the company as a foreman and, after receiving one promotion after another, finally wound up as general foreman of the Bottoming and Goodyear departments. He was an honest man. If he thought you were wrong, he would let you know in no uncertain language. If, on the other hand, he thought you were right, he was just as frank, and he did not care who heard him. He would not hesitate to criticize, condemn, approve, and even praise you behind your back or in your hearing. He was an agitator.

The Importance of Recognition

I remember a discussion I once had with a factory superintendent who said, "I find it dangerous for a supervisor to compliment a worker for anything. It won't be 24 hours before he will be asking for a raise." I could not possibly disagree with anything more. I can think of no example of more complete failure to evidence any understanding of the relationship between psychological values and economic efficiency. Fortunately, so extreme a position is not common. Unfortunately, even those who do not hold it often neglect to take advantage of the opportunities that present themselves for commending the deserving worker. Art Hamilton was one of these.

Art would often say to me about a worker, "H.L., if we had nothing but fellows like him you would not need a foreman," but he made the common mistake—so often made by agents of management—of underrating the importance and advantage of *telling* these boys *themselves* some of the nice things he would say about them to others.

Art knew that workers need praise as much as they need money, even though they may not realize it; that no one can do his best work without the stimulus of recognition; and that disregard of this human yearning is the principal reason why workers find factory work at low levels so ignominious. But even so, Art Hamilton, one of the best foreman I ever knew, would sometimes overlook this most important of all principles of human relations. I remember one incident he never forgot; nor did I.

Early one Monday morning, Art came to my office with Ray (Buddy) Pollnow, one of his Goodyear stitchers. The man's face was a sight to see—that is the small part one could see. His head was in a bandage and a small part of his face, with only one eye, was visible. Art, with a whimsical smile, said, "H.L., Buddy had an accident yesterday and is in no condition to work, but he insists that he is all right and won't go home where he belongs."

This was about 6:45 A.M. (we started at seven those days). I turned and asked Buddy why he wanted to work when it seemed so obvious that he could not be feeling up to it. Art spoke up again before Buddy could reply, "You see, H.L., in all the 21 years Buddy has been with us he has never been late one minute or absent a single day! Now he does not want to break his record."

I was dumbfounded, and I looked upon this small, resolute, and determined man with amazement and incredulity. Before I could find the words to tell Buddy how proud I was that the company had in its employ such a man with such a record, Art continued and told me how Buddy had been injured at a baseball game on the previous day, how his wife

had tried to keep him home that morning, and how Buddy
had insisted on coming to work to keep his record intact. I
could tell by the expression on Art's face that he was proud
of Buddy, as was I. I regretted, however, that it took an incident such as this, before an otherwise superlative supervisor would think to commend Buddy on this remarkable
record—something he should have done long before.

We finally persuaded Buddy to let someone drive him
home, and I thought to myself that many men in management circles had received special honors for records of one
kind or another that required much less devotion to their jobs
than was displayed by this resolute shoemaker. The factories
of the world have many thousand Buddy Pollnows, and seldom indeed does a busy management take the time or have
the inclination to reward properly such acts of devotion to
duty.

In one of our large cities a short time ago, a gala event was
celebrated. This city is the home of a mighty industry, and
in one of its plants a new and modern machine had been
completed. It marked a major technological advance, and a
celebration in honor of the event was justified. The pride of
the managers knew no bounds, and they well deserved the
oratorical tributes paid by dignitaries of the city and many
other leaders. Tributes were also given to the scientific gen-
iuses who had conceived the remarkable mechanism, as well
as to the staff that had so successfully brought the work to
completion. Well and good. *But I listened and looked in vain
for the voice or presence of even one man who had actually
helped to build the machine!*

What must have been the feelings of futility and humiliation of the thousands of men and women of the plant of this
great company as they could hear in the distance the loud
acclaim for those who had provided the plans, the direction,

and the tools, without one iota of recognition for those who, with their strength and minds, had so skillfully used them? Is it any wonder then that a worker's attitude under conditions of such psychological neglect is negative? "Many men can stand to be poor; few can stand to be nothing."

Seniority

Sensitivity to psychological values leads, along with the encouragement of freedom of speech and the generous use of commendation, to a recognition of the great importance to the worker of the principle of seniority. If the older worker has to face the risk of a younger and more active man being promoted to a job that he has been waiting years to get, he is indeed insecure and frustrated. Hence his devotion to the principle of seniority. It is one of the basic factors that sustain the hopes and morale of a factory worker.

I knew Johnny Bates well. He was a heel-trimmer—a semi-skilled job—in our bottoming room. I was a member of our factory bowling league, and Johnny was on the same team. His charming little wife nearly always accompanied him to the bowling alleys. They had no children, and I always suspected that it was because they were waiting until Johnny could get a promotion to a skilled job such as edge-trimming in the same department.

Johnny had been with the company for 14 years, and he was now in line for the first vacancy on the edge-trimming job. This fact, however, was not known to me, and it was far from my mind as I was struggling with the problem of trying to find a way of improving the economic welfare of some of our most skilled workers, without at the same time increasing costs.

The day I heard that Ed Schneck, one of our old edge-

trimmers who had been out on leave, would not return because of his failing health I immediately looked up Art
Becker, the business agent of the union, and said: "Art, why
get someone to take Ed's place? You know as well as I that
the edge-trimmers we still have can easily do the work without promoting someone to take his place. Why not let them
make the extra money?" Art heard me out like a kind father
who listens tolerantly to his son, then patiently explains some
of the facts of life. "H.L.," Art replied, "you can't do that.
We have a man on the heel-trimming line who has been
waiting 14 years for that job. What do you think it would
do to him? And how do you think it would make all the fellows in the room feel to see Johnny Bates denied the opportunity for this promotion he has been waiting for so
long?"

Knowing Johnny so well myself, and knowing his circumstances, as I did, I could see the justice of Art's position. "I
guess you're right, Art; we will promote Johnny," I replied.
Even though I had been a factory superintendent for some
30 years at the time, I went back to my office with a feeling
that this uneducated but very intelligent shoemaker, Art
Becker, who had been serving the union for many years, had
taught me a lesson in human relations that I would not soon
forget.

Art and I did not even discuss the fact that there was a
younger and faster man on the heel-trimming line, who
would have unquestionably learned the art of edge-trimming
more quickly than Johnny Bates. The faster man did not have
seniority, and the question of giving him the promotion on
the basis of merit did not enter the minds of either one of us.

This is not the end of the story. Johnny Bates proved himself a man of more than mechanical ability. After making
good as an edge-trimmer, he was chosen by management on

the basis of *merit* for a supervisory job, which in this organization, and in my judgment, is the only right basis for the selection of administrative personnel.

Restriction of Output

One of the most baffling aspects of factory work, and one of the things least understood by persons without an intimate personal experience with it, is the persistent practice on the part of bench and machine workers of placing a restriction on output. Even plans based on piece-work rates with high incentives attached for exceeding stated quotas have failed to put an end to this practice. Actually, failure to understand it is simply a matter of failure to understand the basic psychological attitudes of workers.

A new employee may enter the modern factory with ambition, a fair amount of education, determination, and high hopes of rapid advancement. If he is fortunate enough to have the talent, training, and aptitude for supervisory or administrative work and the opportunity of demonstrating it to those who are looking for such qualities, well and good. He may go far. He is the exception. But let us look at the situation of the average boy or man, reared in the environment of a working man's home. Suspicious and class-conscious, he is taught the ethics and philosophy of those who believe that labor is a commodity and that man who labors should do as little as he can and get as much as he can for it. He is also likely to be taught that the amount of goods to be made is limited, and only by restricting output can he hope for continued employment.

The new employee is soon told by the workers how much of the operation is a "day's work," and he better "damn well" pay attention and govern himself accordingly. *Such restric-*

tive practices have been made necessary by management's similar attitude of regarding labor as a marketplace commodity.

Workers have long since discovered that extending their strength and stamina to the utmost can and usually does result—after all is said and done—in no more than a "living wage."

The Worker's Attitude Toward His Boss

Although a high degree of mutual trust and admiration often exists between a boss and worker, it is seldom the worker is willing to show his real feelings before his fellows, lest they suspect him of "polishing the apple." While it is easy to understand the psychological reasons why he is reluctant to reveal feelings of admiration or approval toward those in authority, we cannot help but regret the circumstances that have created such an unfortunate relationship. Typically, the worker's attitude would make it seem as if he felt that the best interests of workers can be served only by finding fault as much as possible, rather than expressing approval. Actually, this attitude presents a very unrealistic picture of most worker-supervisor relationships.

And there is another reason why the worker hesitates to let the boss know his feelings of admiration. He believes any expression of satisfaction with the situation would be bound to prejudice adversely any hope of promotion or increased compensation. He can see no reason for a boss being concerned about a well-satisfied employee. He is inclined, therefore, to subscribe to the theory that it is the crying baby who gets the milk.

I was amused to receive a letter many years ago from one of the company's employees located in Edgerton, Wisconsin.

He was serving his country in the far Pacific area during the Second World War and, in the course of his letter, he expressed a warm feeling for his foreman, saying "How is old Fred, anyway?" But quickly realizing that he had let his natural feelings of affection for his boss carry him further than good judgment would justify, he added, "but don't tell Fred what I said." The truth of the matter was that this soldier boy loved "old Fred" and was suffering real nostalgia in the thought of their pleasant factory association. But even this thought could not cause him to ignore the worker's code.

Women in Industry

It is much more difficult to interest the female factory employees in principles of democracy than it is men. On the other hand, they are much quicker to respond to the soft, friendly approach, even though the supervisor using it is strict in his attitude of insisting upon the rules and regulations being faithfully observed. Unlike the usual male workers, factory girls are quick to accept an opportunity of demonstrating their appreciation. It is not unusual, for instance, for factory departments composed largely of women employees to contribute small sums for the purchase of a present for their supervisor at Christmas, or perhaps on the occasion of his leaving them to take another job. This is done in recognition of fair and considerate treatment, rather than for favors extended at the expense of the company, as some cynical factory managers sometimes suspect.

Before succeeding Harsh as superintendent of the Hickory Street factory in 1905, I served several months as foreman of the fitting room, a department consisting of about 200 girls. When the announcement was made of my promotion, the girls presented me with a gold charm for my watch chain.

Knowing Harsh's belief that gifts from workers to foremen were nothing more than attempts to reimburse a man who had been generous with his employer's money, I can only smile today as I remember my embarrassment. Harsh and Johnson believed that I had made a good record as foreman of the fitting room. I had reduced costs and increased production. It was largely because of this record that I had been selected as Harsh's successor. Now the girls had spoiled everything by this gift.

I had no thought of concealing the facts and hurried to Harsh's office, where I expected that at least his advice would be to return the watch charm to the girls. To have received such advice would have been tantamount to an order and would have put me in an embarrassing predicament. I was fond of those girls. They had cooperated with me so splendidly that it was only because of them I had achieved my unexpected promotion. I wanted so much to keep the gift as a remembrance of their friendship.

I think Harsh must have detected a look of great concern on my face as I burst into his office to make my anxious confession. He seldom smiled during working hours, but he was too amused this time over my discomfort to do otherwise. "I know how you feel about this sort of thing," I said to him, "I don't know why they did it. What am I going to do?" "Keep it," he replied, "this is a different kind of thing. You have made friends of the girls in your department while at the same time you have insisted upon their earning their wages." It was a great relief to discover that Harsh could understand that workers could admire and accept the leadership of supervisors that are strict and efficient so long as they are understanding and just.

Because women are slow to take an interest in labor organization their interests are seldom given the consideration they deserve. More often than not, a woman does more work for less pay than her male counterpart, and she finds it difficult to be happy under such discrimination.

A woman factory worker is more sensitive to her status than most people suspect. This has nothing to do with the kind of status that is represented by an organization chart which illustrates the chain of command. The manager outranks the superintendent, the superintendent outranks the foreman, and the foreman outranks the workers on the bench or machine. This matter of relative rank extends even further into all kinds of conceivable situations—the status of a skilled as compared to a semiskilled worker, and so on down to common labor; the employee with long seniority over the newcomer; the articulate and courageous woman or man whom the management may call an "agitator" versus the quiet, timid soul who fears to express his thoughts.

This status is imposed by the attitude of society. It regards the white-collar worker more highly and invests him with higher social status than it accords the factory worker. A new employee in the office, with his white collar and clean hands, has a certain appearance of importance that a new factory hand in his working clothes does not have.

Men and women cannot be expected to ignore the conscious knowledge of the different status of those who work for a salary, under clean surroundings and perhaps in close proximity to higher-ups, and those who work for an hourly wage or a piece-rate, far removed from the man who determines their fate, and who are subject to instant separation from payroll without notice.

It is far from enough to compare compensation. True though it is that the lowest-paid employees in a factory probably earn more than their white-collar counterparts, it is also true that the office worker would never consider changing places, even though it represented an economic gain.

The factory girl may have great skill in operating a machine or in another type of work that is certainly as important and as difficult to learn as her smartly dressed sister who sits at a desk under cleaner conditions. She may have as clean a mind and as good manners and habits. But nevertheless, she can detect on the part of her office acquaintance an attitude of superiority and a quicker willingness to say when asked that she works in the office of the big manufacturing company rather than in the factory.

It is not easy for a woman or a man to accept graciously this imputation of inferiority, and it presents one reason why management has not been able to get from factory employees paid hourly wages the degree of cooperation it has always thought it should receive.

Unless economic organizations are to be plagued with recurrent strikes and disorders by unhappy workers, they must find ways and means to satisfy the human soul as well as to meet the material needs of mankind.

Summary

These ways and means involve simply the abandonment by management of its arbitrary power to make decisions affecting the workers' interest without their consent; the scrapping of the philosophy that labor is a commodity to be purchased at the lowest possible price; a realistic understanding of the restrictive output philosophy adopted by the workers in self-defense; acceptance of seniority, when the worker having it is qualified for the new job, rather than the so-called merit system, which breeds so much social discord; acknowledgment that inasmuch as the Constitution guarantees all citizens freedom of speech, management should see that workers have it on the inside of the plant without fear of reprisal, just as they have it on the outside; inauguration of a system of severance pay, graduated according to length of service, that will ease the blow that comes to every man or woman who loses his job; and abandonment of those detestable practices that make it impossible for a worker to secure employment in a competitive organization without first sacrificing the job he already has.

Unlike the fortunate owner of capital, the man who works by the hour cannot diversify the investment of his only asset —the ability to work. He is forced to risk everything he has in one place. With a job that seldom pays more than a living wage; with needs for food, clothing, housing, and schooling for his children as great as the man of capital; with chances of promotion extremely limited, and unfair restraints used when he tries to secure a better job elsewhere; with the fear of old age and diminishing strength always with him; with constant risk of layoff without notice, or even arbitrary discharge; with inadequate opportunity to communicate with those in authority; and with little appreciation or recognition for good work performed or faithful service rendered, the hourly worker's position is often ignominious and his future insecure.

Yes, Art Strege, there is still today, just as there was forty years ago, a lot of truth in your statement that "A working man can never have any money anyway." But it need not always be so, and will not if men of management, capital, and labor will seek diligently for new ways and means to give to the millions of Art Streges and Buddy Pollnows and Johnny Bateses the status and position of dignity in common enterprise that they rightfully deserve.

8

THE LOT OF MANAGEMENT

The man who heads a large industrial corporation today may well be so busy with the broad policy problems of the business that he never comes in contact with the factory staffs and may never have even seen the factories themselves. In all the years I served as foreman and superintendent of a large factory in St. Louis, I never once knew of the president of the company taking the time to visit one of the company's factories. Not only the president, but sometimes a vice-president in charge of production, may seldom, if ever, see the human beings who actually do the work.

This type of executive has little association with workers. He devotes his time to the men on whom he has placed the responsibility to get things done. How they do it is of little concern. Managers are the important and valuable men in his organization, and he is quick to anger if a competitor dares to entice them away.

The dynamic aspects of business, with its large rewards for success, often lead otherwise good and splendid men into paths of hardness that are entirely foreign to their real character.

How can one reconcile the kind and solicitous private actions of such men with decisions they so often make when wearing their business hat? The executive himself is frequently dissatisfied with attempts to justify his strange double life.

Of course, not every business leader has a different code of ethics in his office from those he holds in his social and home life. There are many business leaders whose natural kindly attitude is not removed like a coat when they enter their offices. The business is fortunate that this is so because policy is made at the top, and if the attitude of the man at the top is an understanding one, it is most likely to become the attitude of middle management and all management.

The mind of the executive head of a business is filled with problems arising from fast-changing economic conditions. He is occupied with the task of properly financing his operations, both for expansion and for current operations. He must keep informed of technological developments that may vitally affect his competitive position. He must know his market and keep a watchful eye on sales, production, and profits. He must also keep up with the world of ideas, both within his own organization and outside. He is keenly interested in legislation, existing or proposed, that may favorably or unfavorably affect his business. Government and legal controls must be accepted and implemented, even though the executive may think they are exceedingly objectionable. Much of his time must also be devoted to personality problems within management.

These various duties and matters that vitally concern his business leave him little time to give personal and intimate attention to problems that may be even more important and that his training may not have qualified him to solve. He is too far removed from human beings at the low levels to understand their psychological reactions. Communication probably ceased long ago. He not only does not understand their feelings and emotions; he probably does not know that he does not understand, and he often tries to cure his troubles by employing efficiency engineers or perhaps by increasing supervision. He reads in the papers about strikes and threatened strikes; about unreasonable demands on the part of leaders of labor; about racketeering and bossism; about picket lines and rowdyism. He becomes sick of unions, union leaders, union workers, and he is probably impatient with anyone who suggests there might be reasons, for which he shares responsibility, for some of the things he does not like.

As business has become concentrated into fewer and larger units, the system of authority, as drawn on a company's organization chart, has become of increasing importance and the source of constant anxiety and conflict. Each echelon of management becomes progressively more aware of its relative rank and status.

Some large industrial organizations may have as many as six or seven echelons of authority, and each group, growing smaller in number as they reach the top, is dependent on one man and his arbitrary will.

As the pyramid of authority gradually converges at the top, the degree of responsibility and the sense of loneliness also reach their peak. Each man in the chain of command is looking upward to the man who gives him orders, who can punish or reward, who sometimes, it seems, expects the impossible, who criticizes him when things go wrong below—things for which often he feels in no way responsible. He looks upward to the only man in the organization who can increase his salary or further his ambition for promotion. So, too, does his boss look upward, until the one man is reached who answers only to a board of directors, which he often dominates.

Each manager in the chain of command, with the exception of the man at the top, must give his principal attention to his immediate superior, who holds the power that may make or break him—who can pass a good or a bad word about him to those above. He becomes a student of his boss's likes and dislikes. It may be an opinion, a mannerism, or a personal habit that his boss is intolerant of, but he must be careful to find out and be careful not to offend. He is not concerned with what the men below him think; his eyes are always on the man above.

One boss cannot tolerate certain attitudes on politics, or types of social behavior; another objects to cigarettes or gum chewing; still another dislikes unshined shoes, dirty linen, or bad breath. The man at the top may be irritated by only one of such things, but his immediate subordinates must change their habits accordingly. They in turn will add one or two of their own biases or peculiar dislikes, so that by the time we get to the lowest rung of the ladder many things that the ambitious young executive must in time learn and learn to accept have accumulated.

The relationship between managers on different levels of authority are likely to be strained by the necessity of each boss not only judging his subordinates by his own standards, but also by the standards of the man above, who may have ideas and standards of conduct somewhat different from his own.

The process of filtering information as it flows from the ranks to the top in a large organization is such that the top man really knows little of what goes on in the shop. Each echelon in the chain of command passes upward as much favorable information as possible—and as little unfavorable. By the time it reaches the big boss, the information is either a greatly exaggerated version of something he will be pleased

to hear or a much watered-down account of something unpleasant.

The head man of the organization is likely to have only a
few men to whom he gives orders and through whom he receives information. These few, however, soon learn what is
expected of them: the policies, the standards of conduct, the
degree of authority, and the responsibility. In some types of
business, their responsibility may extend to external behavior
and even to social activities—all depending on the man at
the top. Any ideas the top man has on proper conduct for
managers in the organization are passed down the chain of
command as each echelon grows larger and larger until the
first line of supervisors is reached.

Because each manager wants so much to impress the
authority above him, managers will attempt at times to anticipate their superior's wishes in order to be credited with
good judgment. The job of impressing the man in authority
above sometimes gets to be more important than the work
itself.

The competition, strain, and tension among members of
lower and middle management, jockeying for position and
promotion, are greater than among workers on the machine
or on the bench. The hours are longer, and in some kinds of
business many managers find they have to take their work
home, or entertain at home for business reasons, and therefore much of their energies and home life have to be devoted
to work. The great mass of men in management find it difficult to save and accumulate enough to provide them with
a secure income after retiring and eventually to make them
independent of their jobs. In many types of business, the
field of management has become as much of a profession as
either law or medicine. Also there is often the great disadvantage that social pressures of status and his normal hu-

man desire to be important require the businessman to live up to the limit of his income in the competitive struggle.

Management has to pay a price for status. A manager often feels the necessity of maintaining a social status with higher-ups who can assist him in his ambitions. True or not, he often feels that he must play the game if he expects to get ahead, and with this handicap, he has less freedom in his private life than the man on the bench. In many fields, management in large organizations finds increasing pressures to entertain business associates at home. Privacy is at a premium.

Management is just as much the victim of the impersonalization of business as are the bench workers. They both suffer from our mass-production economy, which requires specialization and increasingly larger organizations for manufacture and for distribution.

The rating of ability is an arbitrary judgment, usually by one man, and catering to the whims of that boss becomes an absolute necessity. Also, a manager's talents are seldom known outside his company, and even on the inside they are known only to a small circle. The opportunity of securing a position elsewhere is so uncertain that these managers often put up with intolerable working conditions and exploitation of their talents and training. When looking for men to accept larger responsibilities, almost every organization selects on the basis of ability. The length of service is of secondary importance.

In large organizations, the individualist is scarce. The great majority accept the thinking of the group, and the group thinking is that the important things of life are the kind of car they drive, the particular private school attended by their children, from whom they buy their clothes, and whether they belong to the right country and city clubs. It is not surprising that they seldom accumulate savings under such pressure.

Consider the shorter life span of American executives and the high incidence of ulcers and heart trouble among this group. Such physical ills are the result of strains and anxieties that are an intrinsic part of the responsibilities of a manager. Unfortunately, the type of managers who are willing to pay such a price are usually the type that are never satisfied with the status they attain, but are always looking for something more. If they attain economic success, their ambitions are often unsatisfied. They will feel the necessity of excelling in something else; perhaps in art collections, larger benefactions, or more foundations and endowments that will lift them still higher in the field of social status.

The larger size of business organizations brings increasing specialization. This creates a sense of dissatisfaction that applies as much to the specialist management technician as to the worker on the assembly line. This manager, like the bench worker, rarely sees the entire process, and therefore cannot properly assess the contribution that his own abilities have added to the making of the final product, or to the business process in which he is engaged.

The pressure of work, deadlines, and quotas is so intense, and he has such a feeling of responsibility in meeting them, that it becomes increasingly difficult for him to understand the attitudes of people and factors beyond his control. He is so anxious and preoccupied with meeting his targets that it is difficult for him to understand that other people do not have the same interest or concern for his success, and are not inclined to work any harder than union rules permit in order to achieve that which only benefits himself and perhaps unknown stockholders.

He knows that he is judged on merit alone, and yet he

often feels himself at the mercy of men who watch the clock, and who he imagines do not care a hang whether he makes the grade or not. He is expected to do his job well, and he can expect criticism if he fails. To succeed is a matter of course, and recognition and appreciation are not considered necessary. After all, his boss does not consider him a child to be patted on the head when he has accomplished his task. But his soul, like those of his superiors and his subordinates, longs for recognition.

Men in top management usually have the power to name their own compensation. In too many instances, the figure they set suggests that they consider themselves to be exceptions to the rule that no man is indispensable. Sometimes they also have the security of either long- or short-term employment contracts, but when it comes to lower or middle management, such security is practically nil. Men in these classifications do not have the power to set their own salaries and can usually be dismissed at the whim of a superior. Moreover, they have no recourse for the correction of an injustice, such as a bench or machine worker may have through membership in his union.

In the field of management, even more than labor, a business organization will often refuse to consider the application of a man presently employed by a competitor, or by any other organization. A manager who wishes to improve his position by changing employers is accused of "disloyalty" to his class; and should a firm happen to hire him, it is termed "piracy"—grossly unethical conduct in the field of *employer* relations.

While the talents, training, and experience that enable men to rise in the field of management are retained in their fullest to a much greater age than those of the machine or bench worker, managers still find that when they reach some chronological age of retirement, which management has designated for them, they must accept the rigid rule even though they often have retained much energy and ability and practically always a desire to continue with their work.

Women who want to make a career in management seldom have their abilities recognized as quickly and objectively as their male counterparts. They are competing in a male world, which is organized to their disadvantage. A woman is always under suspicion of having a real ambition for home life, rather than for business success. Her superiors tend to doubt her stability and real desire for permanence in the work. Regardless of her value as, say, a really outstanding executive secretary who knows every phase of her boss's job, she usually finds the next step up the ladder in the organization chart extremely difficult. The higher she gets, the fewer men in the higher echelons of management will look upon her as an equal. It is only after years and years of devoted service that she is likely to become more than a minor officer of the company, and it takes a woman of very superior talents to get this far.

Managers are not only judged on their willingness to devote themselves wholly to the job, or on their willingness to subordinate home life and other interests to their work; often it is necessary for them to have the ability to make contacts useful to the business. Their originality, imagination, and bearing are all assets by which they are rated. Their psychological skill in handling their superiors with tact and subtle flattery, their organizational ability, and their political cunning and strategy for getting ahead are all important. There are times, too, when an attractive wife with special social charm will be exceedingly helpful in the struggle for advancement.

Without the security of either the man at the top or the

man at the bottom, forced to conform to policies dictated by the president, and without the opportunity to express thoughts contrary to established policies; dependent on the arbitrary will of one man for promotion or even the continuance of their jobs; with no bells or whistles to notify them the day's work is done; with what often seems to them limited authority and unlimited responsibility, the men in lower and middle management become victims of big organization authoritarianism and need, in some respects, even more of the freedom inherent in democratic processes than do the men they direct.

It is therefore to the interest of men of management, quite as much as to that of men of capital and men of labor, to seek diligently for the principle of *common enterprise;* not only because it promises economic gain, but also because it provides greater opportunity for psychological equilibrium. To be partners in production, to have more opportunity for self-expression, and to participate in the fruits of their labor *directly,* rather than to be only hired men, changes the attitude and behavior of managers as much as it does that of workers.

9

SHAREHOLDERS AND LABOR

Industry is a joint venture of labor as well as of management . . . For the preferential treatment capital has thus far received there is no defence possible on grounds of democratic theory or fundamental justice. If investment in industry has any meaning at all, it is surely one equally shared by the man who gives his labour and the man who gives his capital. The one is a material, the other a human investment. Both are investments, and of the two, the one involving life is the more precious.

These words were written by the Canadian statesman and former prime minister, Mr. Mackenzie King, in 1918. They are even more relevant today, with the tremendous growth of investment capital.

In discussing the problem of shareholders, we must differentiate between the small corporation, usually owned by the management or its family or friends, and the larger company, only a small portion of whose stock is held by management.

The investor in a small new business takes a great risk and deserves a correspondingly large return on his capital. These small businesses, often dependent on the talents and energies of one man, are frequently undercapitalized. More than any other factor apart from inexperience, this inadequacy of working capital and reserves for emergencies accounts for the exceptionally high mortality rate among such new ventures.

However, the vast majority of investors, looking for maximum security, marketability for the shares they buy, and as good a return as possible on their investments, tend to confine their purchases to the shares of well-known and established businesses. They select companies that have a past record of success and are sufficiently large to qualify their securities for listing on one of the country's major stock exchanges. Furthermore, careful investors diversify their holdings and limit their risk in any single organization.

Corporation laws that enable investors to limit their risk in any one company to the value of shares held have been a great boon. These laws have made equity shares of a successful company most desirable. The investor would seldom take the risk if he were forced to assume liability for all the indebtedness of a company in which he held shares. The men in management who know the value of equity in the company sometimes have all the stock they want and prefer to use additional funds they may have for outside investments.

The legal liability of a corporation's board of directors, apart from obeying the laws of the country, is limited to the interest of stockholders only. The stockholder, therefore, except when he is also a part of management, is nothing but an investor and has little interest in the company except to the extent that he wants to know it is financially sound and has a good profit-making potential. When the time comes for election of directors, the great majority of stockholders do not attend the annual general meeting, but sign proxies sent to them for men and measures recommended by management. Those who do attend cannot be expected to have sufficient knowledge of the business to vote intelligently. So while in theory the stockholder owns and controls the business and takes all the risk, in actual practice management, usually controlled by large financial interests holding a minority of stock, runs the business and operates it as it pleases.

The management will distribute a part of profits to the stockholders in the form of dividends, will build a reserve out of surplus earnings, and will often continue to pay dividends in those periods when there may be no profit.

The management and the stockholders, however, often lose sight of the fact that the same hazardous conditions that make success of the enterprise uncertain for the stockholder apply as well to the worker. He, too, takes a risk when he hitches his wagon to the star of a competitive business enterprise. As previously discussed, he cannot spread his risk, as the shareholder does. Everything he has is in the hands of one management. He can lose wages or even his job if management fails. Why, then, should he not benefit from the management's success?

The same principle that justifies management in distributing excess profits to shareholders ought also to apply to the worker. His income should not be limited to a living wage any more than the stockholder is limited to a normal return on money invested.

There are no good years and extra earnings for the worker. His good years are limited to steady work at a living wage, with the exception of an occasional hand-out in the form of a bonus or Christmas gift from a paternalistic employer.

Where the stockholder may have occasional extra dividends, either in cash or stock—melon cuts in the form of two, three, or more shares for one, and sometimes with no reduction in dividends per share—the worker gets nothing.

He has no surplus. When business is bad, he is laid off and has no income. If the business is liquidated, he loses his job and the seniority rights that he may have built up; he may even lose the advantage of knowledge he may have gained in specialized work. If he happens to be over 40 years of age, it will be difficult for him to find another job.

Not only is the stockholder's risk limited to the amount of his investment, but he knows at the time he buys his stock the amount of risk he is taking and what he has to gain or lose through success or failure of the management.

The worker's risk, on the other hand, cannot be forecast. He may be injured or incapacitated at work. He is not a businessman, and he cannot evaluate the chances of being laid off or dismissed. He is often completely at the mercy of a supervisor who may have no better reason for discharging him than wishing to give the job to a friend outside the company. This is rare, of course, but nevertheless, the worker has to take that risk.

In days of economic depression, the shareholder can patiently wait for times to get better. On the other hand, the worker may have given the best years of his life to the business and be dismissed without a single hour's notice.

In the eyes of the stockholder and of top management, neither of whom ever may have seen the worker's face or heard his voice, he is nothing but a commodity that has been purchased for profit, and when no longer profitable, he is laid off or dismissed as though he were a machine that had outlived its usefulness.

This commonly held concept of labor's relation to a business organization seems so inequitable that it is strange that society in general has accepted it without question.

When this attitude of management has been assailed as heartless and cruel, the reply is made that, while it may seem cruel, it *is* business. Business itself is cold. A manager has no right to practice philanthropy at the stockholder's expense. A corporation is owned by stockholders, and only the interests of stockholders should be served. If this attitude is questioned, one is confronted with the statement, "it is only the stockholder who takes a risk, so why should anyone else be considered?"

Some companies have a policy of encouraging their own workers and junior executives to buy stock, usually for two reasons; first, top management believes such equity ownership will increase the worker's efficiency and interest in his job; second, they feel it is a good investment.*

When the marketability of such shares is limited—as for example, with stock of small private companies—even the junior executive is taking a risk, since he may need to cash it in and find no buyers.

Even where the company may have a background of many years of successful operation and uninterrupted dividends, few investment counsellors would advise workers to put their savings in their own company's stock. As an employee, he has already by necessity invested his one big asset—his ability to earn a livelihood by his labor—with his company. It would seem elementary that any small savings he could hope to accumulate should be placed either in a bank or in liquid securities, immediately available for emergencies. If his financial condition warrants buying equities, they should be securities in another company, preferably one manufacturing a different kind of goods or providing a different type of service. Few workers can enjoy much spreading of risk with so many of their eggs already in one basket.

I know from personal experience that stock can be sold

---

* The Nunn-Bush Shoe Company, largely on my initiative, practices such a policy. It has been since my retirement from the business world that my own views have changed.

to employees with the best motives, and conditions can later arise that will cause feelings of deep remorse on the part of the employer. It was so in my own case. A few years after we started our business, encouraged by our early success, we sold shares of preferred stock to employees. In our total absorption in the welfare of our organization, I can see now that we did not give sufficient consideration to this policy, nor did we have the experience necessary to appraise the danger to the workers in investing in a new and small enterprise. We were finding a good local market for the stock, and we had too little experience to realize that it could easily evaporate. This time came all too soon.

The First World War, with its aftermath of spiraling prices, had been a new experience. It never occurred to us that a business might have to face the danger of sudden, disastrous collapse of values.

In the spring of 1920, a gradual decline in business began. While prices ostensibly remained high, we later discovered that, in reality, values were on the brink of collapse. Our continued output of shoes for stock out of high-priced leather, in order to provide our workers with income, was in fact bringing us near to bankruptcy.

Sales of shoes almost stopped. Men continued to wear shoes, and babies were still being born barefooted, but men were digging out their old shoes and having them repaired, while patiently waiting for prices to decline. In our naiveté and anxiety not to disrupt our organization, we had brought the company to the verge of disaster. December found us with something like a million-dollar inventory loss and outstanding notes of nearly three million dollars coming due within six months.

We discovered too late that we had foolishly expanded our profitable and growing business on borrowed money far beyond the point that sound business principles would justify. We were faced with a major financial crisis. We needed all our ingenuity and powers of persuasion to induce our creditors to let us carry on.

Louis Karl, the business agent of the union, approached me one day and suggested the entire resources of the workers might be available if they were needed during the crisis period. Only one worker of the scores owning stock asked the company to purchase his shares.

We did survive. In the first nine months of 1921, we had succeeded in reducing our indebtedness to the point where we were in a sound financial condition. Our credit was restored. We had saved the business, and in saving it we learned a lesson that served us well in the years to come.

There are situations in which distribution of stock to workers would serve the cause of justice. Management at times may serve the interests of both shareholders and workers by withholding the earnings of the business, capitalizing them, and issuing shares of stock rather than cash; but, if the earnings have been in excess of a fair rate of return on capital invested, there is no just reason why the excess should not be distributed among *all* the contributors to production, including those who *use* the tools, rather than *only* those who supply them.

Stockholders and management alone are incapable of either producing goods or distributing them. The same economic conditions that are hazardous or disastrous for stockholders are equally hazardous and even more disastrous for workers. It seems just, therefore, that economic conditions producing profits for those who supply the means of production should likewise make profits for those who furnish the strength and skill to make such means productive.

10

PATERNALISM AND WELFARE PLANS

The most obvious facts are the most easily forgotten. Both the existing economic order, and too many of the projects advanced for reconstructing it, break down through their neglect of the truism that, since even quite common men have souls, no increase in material wealth will compensate them for arrangements which insult their self-respect and impair their freedom. A reasonable estimate of economic organization must allow for the fact that, unless industry is to be paralyzed by recurrent revolts on the part of outraged human nature, it must satisfy criteria which are not purely economic.*

We businessmen who have had the energy, ambition, determination, and, in my case, the luck to attain a fair measure of success in the industrial world find it difficult to understand why men are not always motivated by economic factors alone.

I can understand now, better than I could before leaving the active business world in 1950, the difference in the ambitions and the goals of the man who has, through luck or talent, tasted the sweets of economic success, and the goals of one who has been constantly frustrated in his efforts to raise his standard of living above the level of the masses.

* R. H. Tawney, *Religion and the Rise of Capitalism.*

147

I have come to believe that one of the biggest mistakes in the field of human relations in industry and business in general, in a democratic economic system, is the common practice of attempting to motivate or manipulate the worker through various types of welfare schemes.

Paternalism, charity, and benevolence are virtues much needed in any society, but the motives will always be suspect if associated with a commercial relationship—and particularly so if that relationship is an impersonal one.

In the early days of our company, we were such a small, intimate group that at Christmas time I would personally select inexpensive gifts to give the workers. I would go to each department, have the power shut off, ask the folks to gather around, and hand out the gifts in true Santa Claus style. I knew each of these workers by name, and they thought of the gifts as coming from me personally rather than from the company who paid for them.

This was an unusual thing in 1912. Neither of the companies that I had worked with before going into business for myself had even thought of such a thing, and such a practice was most uncommon.

My friend, Harsh, called me on the telephone one day after he had heard about it and asked me why I did it.

"We have done rather well since we started," I replied, "and we feel grateful to these workers for their good service and want to show our appreciation."

"Oh, hell," he shot back, "you just think you can get more work out of them by doing such things."

I wondered if he was right. Maybe that was the reason. It is difficult to appraise one's own motives. It seemed to me at the time that we did it because of the Christmas spirit. We certainly were grateful and we liked our workers, and I then believed our motive was gratitude, as I told Harsh. Today, my thoughts on this subject have changed, and I now realize there was a dual motive, and that Harsh was definitely closer to being right than I realized at the time.

We occasionally hear of a generous employer who usually owns the entire business himself and who makes exceptionally large gifts and gets big headlines in the papers. He may give each of his employees an automobile, or take his entire force to a resort city in Florida for a vacation.

Such rare acts of generosity toward workers who have served employers well are to be applauded, and no one will begrudge them the pleasure they have enjoyed in the practice. However, I cannot help thinking how much better it would be for society, as well as all the parties concerned, if the workers had received their just share of production as it was produced and could have purchased their own automobiles and vacations. The acceptance of large gifts by an employee from an impersonal source does not add to his dignity nor to his self-respect.

Everywhere, we find companies of wealth and good reputation practicing paternalism, with elements of democracy included, with religious fervor. There are generous men in every country. Such men could not enjoy the wealth they have obtained without sharing with those who have made the accumulation possible.

I once knew an employer who, anxious to have the goodwill of his workers, decided to give them a picnic. In telling about the incident, he said, "I wanted to have a gala event. I paid the wages of each worker for the day. I furnished fine music, the best of food, and all the beer the boys could drink, and do you know what the wretches did? They used the day to organize!"

It never occurred to this man that his workers accepted everything that he considered evidence of his generosity as part of their rightful compensation. To him, they had bitten the hand that fed them. Impersonal gifts will always be suspect.

In our company, it had long since begun to dawn on us that welfare plans, passing out Christmas presents, and giving parties and picnics were manifestations of an entirely false attitude. It was not, however, until the development of the Share-Production Plan that we recognized fully the new relationship and began to look upon our workers, not as inferiors to be coddled and patronized, but as self-respecting men and women who were essential to our organization and related to the management in much the same manner as were stockholders.

Some students of the subject and many business and civic leaders interested in improving management-labor relations have confused the principles of the Share-Production Plan and the concept of a common enterprise with those incentives most commonly used by companies known for their progressive and liberal labor policies.

They are usually based on doing something *to* or *for* the worker within a framework of paternalism. They deserve a more detailed analysis, because understanding of the fundamental cleavage between such plans and the worker-participation system of the Nunn-Bush approach is essential to grasping the meaning of true industrial democracy.

The financial incentive is the most common technique for increasing productivity. Many managers believe that working out a suitable "carrot and stick" scheme is the only requirement for securing a worker's cooperation and inducing him to work to the limit of his endurance.

The simplest form of money incentive is the piece-work system. It is a plan that most managements favor and on the face of it, seems to be one that is the fairest to all concerned.

It is a complicated plan—one that requires expert time study
in order to evaluate fairly the various classifications of work
involved. I never liked it. I never could feel that speed and
quality were natural teammates. While there are many types
of work in which speed can be used without detriment to
quality, there are others, such as the making of fine shoes,
that require care more than speed.

In our own company, we developed a plan that we thought
had the good qualities of the piece-work system without the
drawbacks. We called it the stint system. The management,
in cooperation with the workers' committee, would make up
a schedule that included all the various operations in the
factory. Instead of placing a price on each piece, this schedule would specify the amount of work an operator should
average per day for a specified hourly rate.

We preferred to deal with averages, even though men can
do more work on some days than they can do on others. For
making fine shoes, we felt it an advantage to estimate, in
conjunction with the workers' committee, the average
amount of work a man could do *well,* and to limit him to that
amount, rather than to giving him an incentive to hurry,
possibly beyond the point where quality might begin to
suffer. The workers also preferred this kind of a system, because it tended to create a better social atmosphere in the
workshop.

Bonus Schemes

Bonus schemes are popular with many managers. One of
the popular systems of 50 years ago was to guarantee the
worker a wage per hour based on a certain quantity of work,
and then give him a bonus on a gradually descending scale
for all production over the stipulated amount. Under this

plan, the more work the operator did, the lower the labor cost per unit.

Later, management realized that the more work operators performed, the fewer machines would be needed per unit, and consequently the less floor space, less heat and light, and less supervision—all of which would result in a saving in manufacturing expense that would justify a higher labor cost. So, they reversed earlier plans, which had proven to be failures, and offered higher pay per unit for production over the stipulated amount for base pay. Such plans have proved more successful and are used in some factories today.

A bonus system has also been used as a device to share the fruits of an unusually successful year, when management can have no assurance of its recurrence. Such an occasion offers opportunity to give bonuses to workers when an increase in wage rates might be putting a burden on the business inimical to the interests of both capital and labor. The company may be willing to share with workers profits that have already been made and that otherwise would go to stockholders, but they may not be willing to speculate on the future.

Often, if his factory is organized, a manager will take this opportunity to further his influence with workers and embarrass the business agent of the union. He will, by his action, say "See what I can do for you—something your business agent is helpless to do." Or, if the employees are not organized, he will use such means to impress workers that gifts would not be made if they were in a union.

Such thinking is unrealistic. In the first place, the workers are not fooled, and, secondly, the workers' representative is alienated.

A manager should go to the workers' business agent *first* when he feels a reward of some kind is in order. He should frankly discuss the situation with him, so he can bring up the subject in a formal meeting of management and union and ask for what they have decided is fair. *To give remuneration unasked for is to leave labor wondering if you gave enough. On the other hand, to grant requests for additional pay leaves management with a credit for fair-mindedness that may be reciprocated in the future.*

I recall an incident of this kind shortly after we started working on the share-production principle. We had agreed with the workers that capital should stand the cost of overtime, but I discovered that the office was figuring the premium of 50 percent on the basis of drawings rather than earnings, which made considerable difference. An associate might be drawing $1.75 per hour and earning $2.50. This would increase his overtime pay from $2.63 to $3.75 per hour. It was apparent that the workers had not been aware of this fact and probably would have been satisfied to have the office continue on the drawing rate. I could have easily instructed the office to make the change, but I thought a much better way would be to have the business agent call attention to the fact, thus letting him get the credit for finding the mistake and giving management credit for accepting the union's interpretation. I therefore called the business agent and explained what had happened. He naturally agreed with me and, after consultation with his executive board, he officially called the office's attention to the mistake and the correction was made.

Profit Sharing

Profit sharing, predetermined under a prescribed formula and inaugurated by management without agreement with workers on the justice of the division, is another form of monetary incentive being increasingly used by industry. As a rule, under these plans workers begin to participate in profits only after adequate amounts have been earned for capital.

Under our corporation income tax laws, a company with a government-approved profit-sharing plan does not have to pay an income tax on that part of gross earnings distributed to workers, as it does on that part going to stockholders and the part retained in surplus account. In effect, therefore, each dollar (approximately) paid to workers out of gross earnings is matched by the government through tax saving to the corporation. It is the belief of some corporation managements that sharing with workers some of the excess profits should provide an incentive for the worker to be more interested in the increasing profits and, consequently, in doing more and better work.

Capital Shares Sold to Workers

Another monetary incentive is the previously mentioned practice of management selling stock in the company to workers on favorable terms, sometimes at lower-than-market prices. The results have seldom been satisfactory and have failed to give workers a greater sense of participation. The amount of stock a worker can purchase is too small and the resulting income too little to be anything but a minor percentage of his earnings as an employee. His chief interest will continue to be in his earning capacity as a worker, rather than his dividends as a stockholder.

The Procter & Gamble Plan

Another category of welfare measures now used by large companies to motivate workers I call "paternalism" for lack of a better word. It embraces welfare measures and management-inspired guarantees of wages or employment

Procter & Gamble of Cincinnati, Ohio, has been a pioneer in welfare plans. This company initiated a policy of guaranteed annual employment in 1923. As far back as 1886, Procter, holding a minor executive position, prevailed upon his superiors to give the workers a half-holiday, a practice unheard of at that time. From then on there seems to have been a continuous development of "welfare" labor policies carried out by this company. It was not long before he introduced a profit-sharing plan, death and disability allowances, old-age pensions, and in 1923, a 48-week guarantee of employment. Procter no doubt sincerely believed in humane treatment of his employees, but there is every evidence that he had to be convinced that everything he did was consistent with the well-being of the company.

In the book entitled *Guaranteed Annual Wages,* written by Chernick and Hellickson,* Procter is quoted as having explained how he came to install the guaranteed-employment policy: "The idea came to me one day that, despite spurts and slowdowns in Procter & Gamble business, people use about as much soap one month as another." In 1925, two years after the plan had been announced, Procter said:

> We guaranteed full pay for full-time work for not less than 48 weeks in each calendar year, less only time lost by reason of customary holiday closings or through fire, flood, national strikes, or other extreme emergency. It does not, of course, curtail our right to discharge. And it is limited to employees who, through qualifying for participation in our profit-sharing plan, have proved themselves conscientious and loyal. Our guarantee of 48-week employment removed dread of layoff from our people. They

* From *Guaranteed Annual Wages,* by Jack Chernick and George C. Hellickson, University of Minnesota Press, Minneapolis. Copyright 1945, by the University of Minnesota.

knew, from previous experience with our employee-rela-
tions plans, that when we promised something we'd stick
to it.

Before this policy was installed, the company, it seems,
had shutdowns totaling as much as three months in several
layoffs during the year, and Procter said in an interview at
one time, "After each of these shutdowns, we had lost some
of our regular experienced and valued employees." At another time, when Procter was interviewed about this plan,
he was asked "How does it happen that Procter & Gamble
has gone so far ahead of most firms in giving security to its
workers?" His answer was:

> It's so simple it's really stupid. We went at unemploy-
> ment, you know from the workers' point of view. Some-
> times it seems you get farther if you go at it that way. It's
> all so simple—there's so much soap needed every year.
> Well, then, why not make one-twelfth of that every month?
> And then you can shovel off peaks of your employment
> and fill up the valleys. And it has paid, better than any
> other labor thing we ever did. Paid from our point of
> view—I mean, in dollars and cents. . . . We can't tell
> you in exact figures, but we know it has paid. But those
> are not the big values. The big value is not having on your
> conscience the chap who wants to work and can't find a
> job.

About a year later, Procter stated in a magazine article:

> Recurring periods of unemployment are one of the great
> weaknesses—if not the greatest—in our present social
> system. A mere stoppage for a time of profits, unpleasant
> as it may be, is as nothing compared with the opportunity
> to earn a living withheld from a man who is willing to
> work. The injustice is so great and so evident that industry
> must solve it, or the problem will be taken from her hands
> and placed in those of others not so competent for its
> proper solution.

The Hormel Plan

The George A. Hormel & Company, meat packers, also developed an excellent program for regularizing wages.

In 1929, the Hormel Company had brought out a brand-new product that sold very well. The company doubled and quadrupled its production line and was running three shifts when all of a sudden the balloon burst and Hormel had to lay off its extra help. These men went quietly on their way— all but one man. The man headed straight for the front office and said, "You can't do this to me."

"Can't do what to you?" asked Jay Hormel, then president.

"You can't turn me out in the street. You wouldn't turn a horse out in the street. You can't do it to me."

"You can go back where you came from, can't you?" queried Hormel.

"No!" said the man. "My town has 1200 people. Before I got out of school, I was selling home-popped popcorn out of a basket. I finally got a little stand, selling peanuts, popcorn, chewing gum, and pop. I just got to where I could count on $9 or $10 a week when you sent a man along who said you would pay me $20 a week to help you can your chickens. He didn't tell me you would only keep me a couple of months —just long enough to ruin my business—then turn me out into the street."

I knew Jay Hormel and had discussed these problems with him on more than one occasion. His experience had been much like my own when I had to lay off a great many people about this same time, but he had more difficulty than I did in installing an annual wage plan in his business. His workers seemed to be more distrustful than ours, and it was apparent they had no leadership. They were not organized, and try as hard as he could, it took him several years to sell this new idea to the men who would profit by it as much as the company itself. Jay Hormel was not a hypocrite, and the words that he used in describing his experience to Chernick and Hellickson sound much like words I also heard him say:

> I want to make money, and I am obliged to make money for the other stockholders. I believe the way to make money for me and for them is to make money for you. If the management of this company didn't have that attitude, you wouldn't have a straight-time plan or bonus plan or joint earnings plan, and our wage levels would be no higher than they are in any other packing house.

And at another time, he is quoted as having said:

> The reason it took us four years to get the annual wage idea up to the point where we could even try it, and the reason we couldn't make it work on a plantwide basis as late as 1933, was that we had no set method of talking with the rank and file of our employees. I tried to talk with them. Ask the smokehouse gang if I didn't. I got them in a room and tried to explain the whole thing to them. I got out of the room so they could discuss it by themselves. I tried to do everything I could to give them perfect freedom of action in the matter and to give each a chance to express his own thoughts on the subject. However, no man would express himself freely. Each man had a fear that if he talked too much, and said something we didn't like, somehow he could be penalized. They thought the best way was to take it the way we handed it out, without argument and without comment.

Foodstuff is even more a staple than shoes or soap, and Hormel was in a position to know fairly well how much of his product he could sell in a year. It was true that his sales were not any more regular than those of Procter & Gamble. There were seasons in the years when there was much more slaughtering of animals for meat than there was in other seasons. If he was to regularize their pay into 52 guaranteed payments per year, it was necessary for him to ask his workers to make up for the time lost in dull seasons by working more time in the seasons of the year when production was high. There were times when his men did not work over 24 hours a week, and others when they worked as much as 53. No overtime was paid unless the total hours for the year contracted for were exceeded.

Limitation of Capital's Return

We also have the exceptional man or group of men who operate their business on the extremely rare basis of a fixed rate of return for capital, permitting the labor and management interests to share the rest. Two of the best-known exponents of this philosophy are the Lincoln Electric Company of Cleveland, Ohio, which limit the income of capital to 6 percent and the Glacier Metal Company of London, England, who calculate 7½ percent as a fair return for capital.

This manner of association between men of capital and managerial ability and men of labor has amply demonstrated the heights of efficiency men working for themselves rather than unknown stockholders, enjoying capable leadership and sufficient capital, can achieve. The men who provide such opportunities for labor cannot be praised too highly. However, it is not free enterprise in a capitalistic society. Risk capital too, as well as labor, is entitled to unrestricted income and as a general thing will not "venture" without some prospect of receiving it.

Co-determination

The practice of co-determination in certain parts of Western Germany after the Second World War was an interesting experiment in the field of labor participation in the making of major policies of an industrial enterprise.

It required the placing of workers or their representatives in equal strength with capital interests on the board of directors of industrial companies as recognition of the workers' interest in the enterprise. This program was effected through the efforts of organized labor, not so much for economic gain, but with the thought that it would serve to keep aggressive political leaders from securing the cooperation of industry, as had been the case in the two World Wars of this generation.

Co-determination as practiced in Germany is a step forward in the right direction. However, until labor representatives on the board are selected from among the workers of the company rather than from the officers of national unions, as at present, only the first step has been taken. It may well be that it was necessary to choose trained professional labor leaders at the outset, in view of the fact that the relationship between management and labor on the local level historically has been, at best, a paternalistic one. But unless the next step is taken and local labor representatives chosen from active workers are placed on the board, the German worker will not enjoy the full fruits of real participation.

Consultative Management and Company Unions

Whatever the motive, industrial enterprises in cooperation with labor, sometimes organized and sometimes not, are gradually experimenting more and more with what has come to be known as consultative management. It is a step toward developing the potential of the working man, and it is preparing him for the status needed for the development of a true common enterprise.

As unions slowly gained strength in the inflationary days of 1923 to 1929, there was a large movement on the part of management to stem the tide by themselves organizing the workers of their plants into intramural groups. These groups of employees were financed and dominated by management and designated as "company unions" by national labor organizations. There were no dues to pay, no oaths to take, no expenses to meet. Many of the workers held secret membership in unions of their own choice, but they usually participated in the activities of intramural organizations in order not to incur the disfavor of the management that held so much power over them.

These company unions met on company time and participated in discussions of various innocuous subjects usually brought up by the personnel departments—subjects of a nature that would not be too disturbing to the management.

However, it was a beginning, be it ever so small, of the idea of consultative management. It did improve communication and to the extent that it succeeded in this field it was helpful to the business and to the workers.

Having no real power, their function was limited to an opportunity of presenting grievances in an orderly fashion to higher echelons of management for their consideration and decision.

Progressive supervisors and managers at all levels have learned in the meantime that rich rewards can come, not only from listening to those who direct them, but also from listening to those whom they direct.

General Summary

The small one-man management organization seldom has trouble. The manager is the owner. He hires every employee himself. He works every day in such close proximity to his workers that he knows their names and something about their families. He finds it difficult to treat them as just a name on a payroll or a number on a card.

Such an organization is paternalistic, but in an entirely different sense than the larger organization where workers seldom, if ever, see the face of the man who has so much power over their lives. It is, therefore, this latter type of organization, rather than the small company, that I am writing about in this analysis of industrial welfare programs.

Leaders of powerful countries in eastern Europe and Asia with no respect for political democracy and freedom are making giant steps in their economic development. It is evident that men never having tasted the sweets of freedom will work with more enthusiasm for a state that they look upon as their own than they will to enhance the wealth of unknown stockholders. It is a new challenge, and one that I do not believe we can meet with old methods. Why should workers be asked to accept gratuities with all the humiliating and ignominious implications involved? There is no more reason for stockholders, through management, to give presents to workers than there is for workers to give to stockholders.

The successful business in its external relations is usually an organization of integrity. It may not have at its head and dominating its policies a so-called good or charitable man, but, if it is successful, it usually has men who know the value of ethical business standards.

If, in their internal relations, they seem to be otherwise, it is because of their mistaken concept of the relationship between management and labor.

Many of the liberal policies described earlier in this chapter are admirable as far as they go, particularly those like Procter & Gamble's and Hormel's, which were designed to provide job security. I also believe that we should encourage any programs for the promotion of greater labor participa-

tion in the vital affairs of the business, such as Co-determination, or for the improvement of communications through
formal consultative machinery. I have already expressed my
views on the demeaning nature of welfare schemes and the
unnatural and unjust pressures imposed by the various financial incentives.

But there is a more basic flaw in all these schemes. They
are amelioratives and palliatives. They do not go to the
heart of the problem. It is rather like a doctor prescribing
pills for indigestion rather than advising the patient to eat
more slowly. With the exception of Glacier Metal Company
and the Scott & McHale Shoe Company, not one of these
companies, and many others proud of their progressive labor
policies, has taken the first step of relinquishing its traditional prerogative of arbitrary power, thus acknowledging
labor as an equal and intelligent working partner in a common enterprise. In addition, each of the labor policies was
imposed by management, rather than being jointly inspired
and implemented. Furthermore, the development of bonus
and welfare plans, or even guaranteed yearly employment or
guaranteed annual wages, has not touched another cause of
our industrial unrest: While such plans are sometimes meri-
torious attempts to cure old abuses inherent in the hourly
wage-rate relationship, they do not eliminate the inherent
rigidity in our wage system, nor do they produce the flexibility necessary to keep our economy in balance.

Manipulative welfare schemes, benevolence, and paternalism have no place in a free-enterprise system. Ben Scott,
a worker in the Nunn-Bush factory, voiced at a council meeting many years ago what should be the sentiment of every
working man everywhere when, with his head held high
and in a challenging way, he said, "I don't want anybody's
damn charity."

11

THE ROLE OF THE UNION

The present trade union movement . . . begins with
the faith that the power of the worker lies in collective
action at the economic level. Its decalogue is the contract.
Its prayer book is the strike or the threat of a strike. Its
priest is the business agent.

Labor unions were little known and of little interest in a
small agricultural town in Texas at the turn of the century.
I have no memory of having an opinion on the subject of their
necessity or their conduct at the time, one way or the other.

For some two years after entering factory work, I heard
nothing but condemnation of unions and all their works. All
management men I knew hated the idea that men with no
financial interest in a company had any right to meddle in
the industrial relations of people on the payroll, the prerogative of management only. Labor organizers were looked
upon much as we look today upon communist leaders. What
right did these men have to impose their hostile attitude on
men and women earning their livelihood through employment generously given to them in the shops of industry?
They were agitators—trouble-makers—and were a menace
to legitimate business.

There were no government employment agencies in those

days, no unemployment insurance, no social security, no public welfare. With wages in the shoe manufacturing business running from $2.50 per week for unskilled girls to $18.00 for skilled men, and this for 59 hours of work, workers could not be expected to have savings, and few did. Therefore, when out of work, they had only three choices: beg, steal, or go to the county poor farm.

Under such circumstances, competition for jobs was intense. It was a buyer's market. Many a man lost his job because another man was so hungry he would take it for less. All this time, men of wealth and position, with high social and business standing, could not honestly understand what right men had to organize in a free-enterprise system.

Management hired each employee as an individual and therefore had a right to deal with him as an individual. Management saw no wrong in using spies to locate "disloyal" employees and in using coercion to attain their ends. Discharging an employee, without notice, who was suspected of being interested in union activities was an act of justice.

Most of these employers were good men. They had, in most instances, high ethical standards. Their word was often as good as their bond. They were charitable, good neighbors, and loyal to their friends. But "business is business," and the purpose of business is to make money.

It was shortly after assuming the responsibilities of superintendent of the Hickory Street factory in St. Louis that I had my first opportunity to visit a union shop. For the first time, I listened to praise of unions. The superintendent said it made his job much easier. He made agreements with the union, and every employee was bound to obey these agreements. He had no labor trouble, and he would rather manage a union shop than an open one. I was deeply impressed. As a pacifist by nature, this idea of making agreements to which both sides must adhere appealed to me as a sound approach, rather than the authoritarian concept of dictation by a superior.

Of course, I could not let my boss know that I had the least sympathy for labor organization. He would have considered such an attitude treason to the company. Men with authority and responsibility should have no tender feelings for ideas their superior considered inimical to the best interest of those who paid their salaries. I listened to such statements with an open mind but a closed mouth.

I knew what it was to want work and not be able to find it. When I was a young man of sixteen, economic conditions were bad. I would go to place after place and even ask to work for nothing, hoping to serve so well I might expect compensation in the future.

Like most businessmen my primary concern from the time I entered business until I retired from the world of commerce, 56 years later, was always the welfare and security of my family and myself. Even so, this early experience may well have caused me to have a better understanding and even sympathy with the problems of those who were dependent upon others for jobs. I was fast learning the problem of a worker's factory life, and I did not like what I saw.

The head of an important industrial company once said to me, "Unions have never been able to organize *my* plant. I want no outsiders telling me how to run my business. I have kept them out by beating them at their own game. I keep posted on the wage scales in union shops, and I always pay more. I give my workers a longer vacation, more holidays, more health insurance, larger bonuses—in fact, I always keep a step ahead of them so they never have a chance to tell our people there is something they can get for them that they do not already have in greater measure."

When workers in an open shop receive higher wages or get better working conditions, they should realize such favors are often given by their employer because of fear of a union, and they might be withdrawn just as quickly if the threat were removed. Practically all progress made by leaders of organized labor has been by bitter struggle on the picket line and, in late years, through occasional legislative action. Organized business, as represented by such groups as National Chamber of Commerce, National Manufacturers Association, and business trade associations of all kinds has usually been bitter and universal in its hostility and unrelenting opposition. We can expect and have no right to expect anything but unrelenting hostility in return.

Distrust naturally begets distrust. Arrogance and hatred of organized labor will develop arrogance, hatred, and irresponsibility on the part of labor leadership.

Such a system of unfettered power is seldom voluntarily surrendered, and even today many an industrial management will take any course that gives hope of frustrating union organization activities. Wages will be increased, profit-sharing plans devised, improved working conditions installed, music through loudspeakers provided, picnics, parties, bonuses, gifts given; management will use any and every device that will spare them the odious task of dealing with an outside professional labor spokesman.

Many times I have seen desperate workers, poorly organized, forced by economic necessity settle their differences with management for only verbal promises that could be quickly repudiated when business conditions would enable a manager again to dictate terms.

At no time up to the present day have I seen any appreciable evidence of management as a class really accepting in good faith the right and the advantage of labor solidarity—

no matter how much they might give lip service to the principle of labor organization.

It took real courage in the early days of union organization for a working man to join a union. He could never know when his boss, with spies and stool-pigeons, might discover the fact. In pre-Wagner Law days he was not only discharged immediately, but in most instances black-listed as well.

It was this inhumane and intractable attitude of business management that led to the passage of the National Labor Relations Act of 1935, popularly called the Wagner Act. This Act brought to labor a means of security they had never known before. The Act strengthened the legal position of labor to such an extent that management has been forced to express its hostility in more subtle ways.

There are employers and managers who recognize the need of workers to pool their tiny individual strength, and their need and right to employ articulate men, trained in the art of negotiating, to speak for them. We also have many men in labor leadership who are quick to respond in kind to such an attitude—able, incorruptible, and dedicated men whose names seldom appear in the press, and who would be a credit to any vocation or to any profession.

I remember so well the experience of a friend of mine who was in the tanning business. It was a family business and was then being operated by sons and grandsons of the founder. They were all fine men, and the business was not so large that they were compelled to be out of touch with the men who did the work. They paid good wages, and the conditions must have been better than average because they never seemed to have any labor trouble.

However, a short time after the National Labor Relations Act was passed, the organizer of the Leatherworkers' Union, affiliated with the strong CIO, managed to get a majority of the workers to sign up for membership, and my friend, under the provisions of the new law, could do nothing but accept the union's request for a conference to discuss some of the workers' ideas for changes.

In telling me about the conference, my friend said that these were the first union leaders with whom he had ever come in contact and that, instead of their having "horns" as he had fancied, he was pleasantly surprised with their reasonable attitude. In fact, after the conference he turned to the principal spokesman of the union group and frankly told him so. The man, obviously pleased with my friend's compliment, smiled and replied, "The reason you think we have been reasonable is because you have been reasonable yourself. If you had taken the kind of position employers usually take with us, you, too, would think we were pretty tough."

The fundamental concept of labor organization is democratic; the power at the grass roots, elected officials, responsible to those who bestow the office and its authority and responsibility upon them. It is only as labor organizations have departed from this democratic concept that they have become the just target for criticism and condemnation.

One of the union's major problems is to secure dedicated and incorruptible men at low salaries to administer union affairs on either the local or national level. A union business agent has power, but seldom as much as industrial leaders sometimes think. Contrary to some opinion a union leader seldom has the power to induce men to cut themselves off a payroll and walk for weeks and months on a picket line with only the hope of a few-cents-per-hour increase in pay. Workers know even better than their critics that they will probably lose more money in the process than they can hope to gain, even though they win the fight. Strikes seldom occur except when social and psychological conditions, rather than economic, are the real basis of the discontent. Money alone will not satisfy entirely the unhappy and discontented employee, who deep in his heart yearns to tell someone in authority that he is sick and tired of having to implement arbitrary decisions made by another man.

Business executives steeped in authoritarian practice and fighting the right of labor to organize have toughened the hands of those they fight and have caused them in desperation to use the weapons they find most effective. We should not be surprised, either, that unscrupulous men of ability with compelling love of power have managed to infiltrate the ranks of organized labor leadership.

The labor leader who feels he has vested interest in conflict is taking a short-sighted view. To sit on the *opposite* side of the bargaining table and act the part of a seller of labor may seem a more important function to men who have in the past taken orders from an arbitrary boss, but to experience the thrill of cooperation as equals in a common enterprise has its compensations.

Under *any* system of cooperation, workers need their solidarity and they need experienced and well-trained leaders. The difference is that under a common enterprise concept the leader must be trained in the art of cooperation, rather than in the art of bargaining. He will find it more profitable for himself as well as for those he represents.

As long as leaders of industry insist upon their present omnipotent and authoritarian concept of business organization, and business leadership gives only lip service to the right of the worker to pool his weak individual strength and persists in fighting labor's solidarity, *the strong national and international labor unions will and should live to fight for the rights of the common man.*

It has been a matter of deep disappointment to me that organized labor leadership has almost invariably taken an antagonistic attitude toward the Nunn-Bush concept of a common enterprise. I recognize the danger of what could happen to labor in a close association with management representing capital interest and without the protection of a strong national union. However, this protection does not have to be withdrawn simply because of mutuality of interest between labor and management instead of the usual conflict, as has been demonstrated in the operation of the Scanlon Plan. While this plan does not recognize the complete correlativity of interest between capital and labor as does Nunn-Bush, continued demonstrations of cooperation and successful operation of such a concept will encourage managements to see more clearly the advantage to capital and themselves of labor solidarity. A common enterprise cannot exist without labor solidarity, any more than a stock company can exist without stockholder solidarity.

I agree with Kermit Eby, Professor of Social Sciences at the University of Chicago, who said:

> The only men who can be trusted with power are those who are willing to give it up. And the only organizations which can be trusted are those which have built in them, either by precedent or constitutional provision, the machinery for the orderly transfer of power.
>
> Recognizing men's unwillingness to give up power, and organizational tendencies to self-perpetuation, I would invite the labor movement to amend its constitutions to place limitations on the length of officer's tenure; to incorporate in the election provisions for contested elections; to make possible selection of candidates by petition; to prohibit employees of the unions as convention delegates, permitting only the so-called 'rank and file,' the members, to represent themselves.

The faith of labor in a common enterprise would not be in "collective action at the economic level," as stated by Gus Tyler in *A New Philosophy of Labor** and as is so necessary today, but in collective action as partners in production. Its decalogue would not be the contract alone, but one inspired by the spirit of cooperation; its prayer book would not be the strike and threats of strike, but judicial processes. Its "priest" would not be the aggressive business agent who, with vivid memory of past ill-treatment and oppression, demands of the employer with provoking arrogance that he "sign or else," but a well-trained, diplomatic personnel director, selected and paid by *both* management and workers, who can with dignity and firmness insist only on equality and justice before the law.

* Gus Tyler, *A New Philosophy of Labor,* Center for the Study of Democratic Institutions Occasional Paper.

12

THE NEW ROLE OF MANAGEMENT

The dogmas of the quiet past are inadequate for the stormy present. We must think anew, we must disenthrall ourselves.

ABRAHAM LINCOLN

The principle of labor compensation the Nunn-Bush Co. discovered in 1935 is so important that I believe that it would revolutionize our free-enterprise system if it were generally accepted by men of capital and men of labor.

It gives the individual worker a sense of dignity usually found only in those who are in business for themselves; it enables management and labor to work together in an atmosphere of mutual trust and respect; it provides the worker maximum security and regularity of income; and at the same time it gives to management that flexibility which is at times so necessary to avoid business losses.

Businessmen are conscious of the difference in the attitude of the average wage-earner, using the tools of production, and the average man in business for himself. Few are aware, however, of the correlation of interest that really exists between those who own the tools and those who use them, and the remarkable results that can be achieved by the change in attitude that this knowledge effects.

173

Eddie Zygalowski was not a factory worker. He had the body of a professional football fullback and the spirit of a boy. His regular job was collecting life insurance premiums from people of small means who were only able to make such payments in weekly or monthly installments. The work was easy, limited to regular hours. It left him with lots of time to play, and Eddie liked to play. He had a natural musical ear and could play the piano for hours, though he had never taken a lesson in his life. He liked to dance, swim, roller-skate, bowl, and attend parties; he loved people, and he enjoyed life. Nevertheless, Eddie felt the need of more income and, above all, the need of a more dignified position in society. One day one of his friends who owned a small business offered to sell it on such favorable terms that Eddie, seeing an opportunity to fulfill his ambition, became a businessman.

The business was a one-man establishment. In the front was a counter at which stood a few stools, and behind the counter were a grill and the boxes of buns and meat for the hamburgers that were his principal stock in trade. In the rear were several pool tables. Eddie was in business. He opened up his hamburger stand at ten in the forenoon and closed it at two in the morning—seven days a week.

There were no more parties, no more piano playing, and no more swimming. If I wanted to see Eddie, I was obliged to go out to his place of business and talk to him while he toasted his buns and cooked his hamburgers, 16 hours a day, seven days a week. His wife ran his errands. He missed the old pleasures, but he enjoyed even more the status he had gained, the excitement and uncertainties of business, as well as the better prospects of security for his and his wife's old age. As an employee, he had felt no urge to help increase the profits of the unknown stockholders, even though he himself would gain in the process. As a man of business, he was serious, ambitious, and determined to let nothing stand in his way.

This example of what change of status could do in the way of altering one's attitude was often in my mind as I would invite workers to visit me in my factory office on the occasion of their second anniversary with the company. It was at this time under our cooperative plan that they became associates rather than employees. This was the time they changed their status from wage-earners to sharers of production. "Come in and sit down," I would say, "How does it feel to be in the shoe business for yourself?"

True enough, these men were engaged in group effort and could not expect the same degree of exhilaration that Eddie Zygalowski experienced. Nevertheless, their status did change, and to the extent that the situation was explained and the facts understood, they prospered, the enterprise prospered, and society in general prospered.

Capitalism, with its system of incentives, its spirit of competition, and its rich rewards to those who can reduce costs and improve methods, has developed leaders of great talent. The result has been a standard of living in this country unmatched in all the world.

Even so, the system is not perfect. Reluctance to recognize the mutuality of interest of capital and labor has been its greatest failure. We can have the advantage of such a system, with its resulting economy in the field of technology, mass production, purchasing, and distribution, without the constant and increasing conflict between management and labor.

Free enterprise can be greatly fortified by our accepting in fact, rather than with tongue in cheek, the declaration of Congress in 1913 entitled the Clayton Act: "The labor of a human being is not a commodity or an article of commerce."

Because capital will refuse, without adequate reward, to assume the risk involved in private enterprise, and because management will demand compensation in keeping with its talents, experience, and ability, labor can never hope to receive anything more than a fair share of the values it creates. To demand and receive *more* reduces not only profits for capital and managerial remuneration, but eventually labor's own income and opportunity. To receive *less* is to submit to exploitation.

As business operates today, labor's income is limited. A man is hired on the market much as an inanimate commodity is purchased. In their humiliation and resentment, workers in turn limit their production and take little or no interest in the enterprise. Bound together, either in formal or informal groups with a common interest, they seek to improve their lot by demanding increased wage or piece rates. Little do they understand, indeed little more do many industrial managers understand, that raising wage and piece rates does not necessarily increase a worker's income. To receive frequent increases in wage rates has delighted the worker and in his mind has been the vital factor in his quest for a higher standard of living. Instead of operating as a means of increasing labor's standard of living, it has given labor leadership a potent weapon in their work of organizing. Just as industrial managements have often advanced prices with no concern for what it might mean for the labor interests if higher prices led to decreased production, so have organized labor leaders, in labor's need for solidarity and constant recruitment, often forced wage-rates higher than the public (not the management) was willing to pay.

The cost of labor in calculating the total cost of goods is based on the *rate* at which labor earns its compensation, not on the indeterminable amount of compensation itself. The real income of labor, like the earnings of stockholders, is determined solely by the amount of production and the amount the public is willing to pay for it.*

If businessmen would only accept in good faith the need and right, and indeed the advantage to capital, of worker solidarity, and assist their workers to organize rather than put every possible obstacle in their path, the constant fight for increased wage-rates by aggressive labor organizers would not be necessary.

In reviewing our nation's place in the contemporary world situation, we find ourselves with a destructive internal conflict between capital and labor, and a serious external challenge from a strong and proud nation led by talented men, with its people spurred by fear and its policies enforced by power.

In our country, the internal conflict between capital and labor has become increasingly serious and a menace to the continued superiority of our free-enterprise system. Disagreements are usually terminated not by proof of who is right, but through a demonstration of who is the stronger.

The managerial prerogative arbitrarily to make final decisions, including the act of separating an employee from the payroll, continues to exist in theory. But since the passage of the Wagner Act in 1935, there has been a steady erosion of these so-called prerogatives. This is evidenced by the ever-increasing demands by organized labor and their acceptance by management as subjects for arbitration. Some of the first labor agreements made by management and labor after the passage of the Wagner Act in 1935 consisted of as

---

* Example: If it takes an average of two man-hours to make a certain article at a cost of 2.50 per hour, we must figure a labor cost of $5.00 in arriving at our selling price. And this is true even though the worker himself makes only 50 cents per hour for his week's work because he worked only one day.

few as 15 pages; today, some of them run as long as 139 pages. The matters in which management arbitrarily can make the final decision are constantly being reduced.

Our external problem is to meet the challenge of an authoritarian ideology, conceived in fear and grown strong economically through struggle with an unfriendly world.

When Allen Dulles, head of the Central Intelligence Agency, speaking before the National Chamber of Commerce in 1958, made the statement that the U.S.S.R. was exceeding our rate of increase in production by some 11 percent, it gave this country a shock that promised for a time to rouse us out of our complacency. We find it difficult to realize that a backward country could seriously challenge our superior knowledge in the field of science, technology, and general industrial know-how. No matter how unpleasant, the facts are incontrovertible, and there is general recognition now of our need to find a solution to the problem. We must stop thinking in terms of the past and realistically face the future.

The objective of all industrial organizations should be to produce goods the public needs, and to do so efficiently. This means that good quality and low cost must be maintained, while fair and adequate profit is earned for those who supply the capital. Equally necessary for the common good are safe and satisfactory working conditions for all those engaged in the enterprise. To this end, an understanding is necessary between management and the union, not only on the economic needs of labor, but also on the social and psychological factors necessary to the contentment of men and women engaged in specialized work. Such work is often monotonous, often performed of necessity in unpleasant or dangerous surroundings, and usually devoid of mental interest.

"My business," said Henry Ford, speaking for management, "is to supply economical transportation to the public and to maintain good wages to the workers while doing it. If I can succeed in doing this, the stockholders of the company will never have reason to complain of their dividends."

As long as industrial managements insist on retaining arbitrary totalitarian power, independent, intramural, or independent one-company unions will find themselves powerless to attain a position of equal strength with capital interests, or to settle disagreements by judicial processes. Consequently, the unions must combine on an industry-wide or other broad basis in order to protect their interests effectively against management.

Of course, the Nunn-Bush experiment is not the ultimate solution, but it undoubtedly does contain many of the ingredients of an ideal common enterprise.

By replacing dictatorship with democratic leadership, management can develop mature, interested, and cooperative workmen—men and women with an attitude of respect and trust in leadership, rather than fear, suspicion, and distrust.

The man who in the past has dictated policy should in all humility concede his fallibility and constantly remind himself, as well as those he directs, that the lowest-paid worker has as much right to his own opinion as he does. This is particularly true in those areas where the worker may well have more knowledge than the manager; and inasmuch as the manager does not hesitate to express an opinion on matters about which he is insufficiently informed, he should not complain if others sometimes exercise the same prerogative.

The manager should erase from his mind the old, worn-out, conflict-breeding concepts of an authoritarian, paternalistic, or manipulative relationship. He should banish the idea that it is only through fear or even gratitude that men can be expected to perform best. He should realize that the whole man goes to work only when he feels secure and has his self-respect and dignity. He should insist that the workers have their solidarity so they can feel strong and secure. He should want them to have good leadership from men trained to lead. If such men have had training in the ranks of organized national unions, so much the better. The individual worker should not be considered a hand waiting for orders from his boss, but a deputy from a secure, solid group with whom management is working in a common enterprise. Such a climate will bring satisfaction and profit to those who create it and success to the business they direct. After all, the principle of human relations practiced by Nunn-Bush are nothing more than principles that have been taught by psychologists for many years.

How can labor's suspicions be overcome? By management laying the cards on the table, face up. A cooperative plan cannot succeed unless there is mutual trust and confidence. One partner cannot have secrets from the other. Leaders of industry and leaders of labor must not continue to "relive the past and back into the future."*

After the right social and psychological climate has been created, it is much easier to make gains in the economic areas, and not only for the interests of labor and capital in the enterprise, but for the welfare of all society.

This better relationship, established universally, between capital and labor will enable us to eliminate injurious conflict between two vital elements of the free-enterprise system. We can provide flexible and ample income for labor, as well as for capital, enabling management to adjust prices

* An expression used by Clinton S. Golden.

quickly up or down to meet changing conditions—prices that consumers would be more willing and able to pay. We can also eliminate booms and depressions as well as alleviate unemployment.

We need something more than mere cooperation between capital and labor. To retain a rigid and inflexible wage system is to destroy the partnership concept. For labor to be denied a fluctuating as well as an unrestricted income such as capital enjoys is to lose the great advantage to the national economy that such flexibility would provide.

The principles of democracy are something much too fundamental and much too concerned with the spirit to be imposed overnight by authoritarian edict. Progress toward unity of effort in a democratic common enterprise will be made only when the following principles are accepted and practiced:

1. Executive power should be limited and responsible to a joint board composed of an equal number of representatives of capital and labor, with agreement that representatives of the public will be added to mediate and to act as arbitrators where necessary.

2. While the joint board should be the highest judicial body in finding solutions to management-labor relations, production committees should also be elected democratically in each department to cooperate with management in the interest of all.

3. Labor should be organized without restraint. Management should aid their workers in achieving this solidarity so there can be no dissenting voices after agreements are made. Such unions should have complete autonomy. Democratic principles in labor organizations, as in any other organization, can be main-

tained only if the leaders are responsible to the workers who compensate them for their services.

4. A wise management will assist the union in the task
of collecting union dues through payroll deductions
by agreement with the membership.

5. Both capital and labor should have the advantage of
national associations in order to have the opportunity
of sharing information and ideas, as well as for any
other purpose not inimical to the public interest.

6. No individual in an industrial organization should
have the power arbitrarily to discharge another person. Such action breeds discontent, fear, and hatred.
Experience has shown that workers themselves are
even quicker than management to condemn the vio-
lations of rules jointly made and democratically implemented.

7. Experience has also shown that the worker has no
desire to participate in the making of decisions in
those areas where he has little or no knowledge of the
subject. He can, and should, be consulted on those
problems where he does have knowledge and where
he can make an important contribution to their solution. Such a procedure is not only often profitable to
the enterprise, but always adds dignity and self-
respect to the individual.

8. In a common enterprise, all rules and regulations
should be mutually agreed upon—not bargained for
or imposed by an arrogant union or by a dictatorial
management.

9. Labor should have a just share of the value it helps
to create. Because we can have only what we produce,
and because its value is fluctuating, labor's remuneration should not be fixed and rigid, but flexible and

based on the value of production as determined by actual sales of the product.

10. Because the working man usually does not have resources sufficient to finance his daily cost of living, he should be given a drawing account based on the importance and quantity of his individual production. The workers themselves should take part in the determination of these amounts after agreement with management on the sums that can be safely distributed without danger of exceeding minimum earnings of labor.

11. Drawings should not exceed earnings, and in order that labor can be assured of regularity of income, a surplus should be accumulated in good times to prevent a reduction of drawings in times of low production.

12. The apprentice or worker with a short service record is not entitled to the same degree of security, regularity of pay, or total income as those who, by their length of service and constant loyalty to the enterprise, have earned the rank of "associates," rather than "employees." Acceptance of employees into the ranks of associates should be determined by the joint board.

13. No organization is complete without a retirement or pension plan that will provide security for old age. It should not be installed by management as an incentive plan nor as the product of collective bargaining. The plan should be initiated and designed by the workers with the cooperation and assistance of management. Regardless of how it is financed, it should be made clear to every worker that it is his money that is being used to pay the bill, rather than money donated by the capital interests of the business.

14. Pension plans should not be used by business as a device for securing continuity of service. Plans that tie a worker to one company are unfair when they have provisions that cause loss of maximum benefits if he should leave during his most productive years. It is best, therefore, to inaugurate and administer such plans jointly. They should be accepted through democratic processes and administered by mutual agreement. Pensions should be the personal property of the worker and the provisions of the plan should leave him free to take a job elsewhere without loss of any equity he may have.

15. Elderly men may not want to retire from active work. Although they may be slower in movement, they have experience and skill and often a stronger feeling of attachment to the business than younger men. Such men should not be required to leave, but should be retained without expectation that they can maintain the fast pace of the younger men. They should be given a reasonable amount of work to perform with reasonable remuneration until such time as they voluntarily retire.

With *both* management and labor conscious of a mutuality of interest, with the utmost security for all who give their loyalty to the business, with recognition by the head of the enterprise that each worker has the same desire to be important as he himself has, and with the means provided for each to fulfill his ambition, we can look forward with confidence to a future enterprise system invulnerable to enemies abroad or within our borders—a common enterprise in which each beneficiary, stockholder, worker, and consumer can participate with pride.

Appendix A

STATEMENT OF
ASSOCIATE'S SHARE OF NUNN-BUSH PRODUCTION

FOR MONTH OF June, 1960

Clk. No. & Name......No. 1....John..Doe..Yearly Differential $...3868.80......

Hours Worked...182.9...... Hourly Earning $..2.61.........⎰ Overtime Premium Pay ....$ 6.42.......
(Excluding Overtime Premium Pay) ⎱ Your total earnings for month ....$ 483.65.......

Pairs produced for month 62081......... Average price per pair $...13.64....

Value of production ....$ 843,957.13
Less cost of raw material ....$ 353,871.22
Added value ....$ total earnings $ 490,085.91

Additional Credits ⎰ Group share of upper leather saving $2271.64 ⎱
⎱ Additional overtime credit   427.15 ⎰ $2,816.26
Miscellaneous   117.47

Total Earnings for period ....$ 181,697.62
Deduct hourly wages paid Class HA, HB, C and D Workers ....$ 21,865.23
Balance earned by associates ....$ 159,832.39
Total drawings of associates (excluding overtime premium pay) ....$ 113,934.50
Excess of earnings over drawings ....$ 45,897.89

Your Individual Earnings, Drawings, and Reserve Fund

Your reserve as of .... May 31, 1960 ....$ 1098.91
Cash paid you with last statement .... July 12, 1960 ....$ 131.71
Balance Reserve as of .... May 31, 1960 ....$ 967.20
Your share of earnings (Excluding Overtime Premium Pay) ....$ 477.23 ...... Interest $2.52
Deduct Drawings for sick leave ....$
Deduct earned drawings (Excludes Overtime Premium Pay) ...$ 340.19 $ 340.19
Excess of earnings over drawings ....$ 137.04
Your Total Reserve ....$ 1106.76
Reserve you contracted to keep (25% of yearly differential)......................$ 967.20
Balance ....$ 139.56
of balance withheld to build reserve $ 0.00
$ 139.56

To figure your earnings for month, multiply the "balance earned by share production workers" by the amount of your earned drawings (excluding overtime premium pay), and then divide this amount by "Total drawings for Share Production Associates."

Appendix B

RETIREMENT PLANS

It was not until 1917, five years after the organization of the company, that the management of Nunn-Bush began to think of a plan that would provide some security for its workers after long service. As the years went by after our successful start, we began to realize that to add to the worker's income and security might increase our own earnings and surely would increase the stability of our organization.

Having been impressed with the success of a plan introduced into the Sears-Roebuck company several years previously, we adopted many of its features for our first effort in the field of retirement plans. To add something more than wages to a worker's income in order to secure his cooperation was an exciting new experience. We called it the Nunn-Bush Savings and Profit-Sharing Plan, and its stated purpose was to "encourage thrift and reward long service." Membership in the plan was voluntary. The member contracted to have 5 percent of his wages withheld by the company and placed with the treasurer of the fund, who in turn credited the member's saving account. At the end of the fiscal year, the company would contribute 25 percent of its net earnings to the fund, and a pro-rated share of it would be credited to each member's profit-sharing account—less 10 percent that was held in a reserve to provide for possible decline in the value of securities in which the fund was invested.

The fund was put into common and preferred stocks as

well as high-grade bonds recommended by reputable investment advisory services.

Members of the fund were privileged to withdraw their savings, plus 7 percent interest, without notice, but if they did so before ten years' service with the company they would forfeit any profits in their account. These forfeited profits would be held by the treasurer and redistributed to remaining members of the fund at the end of the year.

After serving the company for ten years, members could withdraw their savings, plus 7 percent interest and profits, without penalty. Each year the member was given a statement showing the condition of his account.

All went well until the financial panic of the early thirties so reduced the value of securities in which the fund was invested that the reserve of 10 percent was entirely too small to cover the losses.

Because of the trustees' fear of further declines, we decided in January, 1933, to liquidate the fund and pay each member the amount that had been apportioned. This action was made possible by the company contributing an additional $40,000 to make up losses caused by depreciation in the value of securities.

In November, 1935, after discussing the matter with our workers and receiving their ideas and wishes, we inaugurated a new plan, which was called the Nunn-Bush Profit-Sharing and Retirement Fund. This plan, unlike its predecessor, had no provision for savings and, also unlike the former plan, included every employee from the president down.

The amount of the company's contribution was determined by a fixed formula as follows:

> 35 percent of that portion of profit-sharing income (before taxes) in excess of $500,000 but not exceeding $800,000; and

40 percent of that portion of profit-sharing income (before
taxes) in excess of $800,000 but not exceeding
$1,000,000; and

50 percent of that portion of profit-sharing income (before
taxes) in excess of $1,000,000.

This arrangement served as a means of capital's sharing
with the workers the fruits of profitable years. It also reflected the acceptance by capital interests of the principle
of a fifty-fifty division of earnings after they had received a
good return on their investment.

The worker would begin to receive credits on his retirement fund as soon as he had been with the company for one
year. When he had served five years, his vested interest at
that time was only 4 percent of his credits. This percentage
of vested interest increased each year until it became 100
percent after his serving 20 years.

A member could withdraw his retirement fund, regardless
of his vested interest, only on retirement, and even then only
if he was at least 50 years of age. For women, the minimum
age was 45.

All money credited to associates and employees in which
they had no vested interest was forfeited if they severed
their connection with the company. It was retained by the
trustees to be reapportioned to remaining members. Thus
each year, in addition to contributions by the company,
there were additional amounts to be apportioned.

The first Nunn-Bush Profit-Sharing and Savings plan was
conceived in ignorance and liquidated in desperation. Membership was entirely voluntary and, while it did encourage
thrift in those who were strong enough to deny themselves
5 percent of their earnings each week, it afforded no protection whatsoever to those who needed it the most—those who

were not strong enough to practice this self-denial. Therefore the plan had inadequate membership.

The 10 percent reserve proved pitifully insufficient to
withstand the financial debacle of 1929–1933.

The second plan was based on experience and has with-
stood the test of time. I only wish that it could be financed
through a reputable life insurance company and a worker's
vested interest taken with him when he leaves his job to take
another. The worker should be given the opportunity of taking a better job when offered without sacrificing any of his
vested interest under a retirement plan.

When the time arrives that a man or a woman is compelled to give up the work of a lifetime, it makes little psychological difference whether he is the president of the company or a worker on the bench; he is relinquishing a job that
was his—a possession that is gone forever.

However, there is usually a considerable difference in the
economic situation. Managers are increasingly adding to
their security through contracts that call for continuous payment of an amount not much less than past remuneration for
as long as they live after retirement. Men and women who
have spent many years at benches and machines need this
kind of protection much more than managers, because they
had much less opportunity to accumulate savings out of their
earnings.

The first charge on the receipts of any profit-seeking organization is of necessity the wages and salaries of the workers and managers, and as long as our present system of limit-
ing labor to a living wage exists, the second charge should
be retirement income for that portion of personnel whose income is so limited they have no opportunity to provide for
old age themselves.

The first charge is met by every management through obvious necessity. It is a good management that also makes provision for the second charge by providing a retirement income for workers before making such provision for managers and before calculating profits for the owners. This is not to deny the right of high reward for venture capital; it is only to insist that human rights take precedence over capital rights.

Our free-enterprise system should increasingly recognize this need before it is too late. It is dangerous for a democratic government to remain complacent with some 16 million citizens of our country now over 65 years of age, two out of every three of whom have less than $1,000 per year on which to live.

Appendix C

Names and terms served by the

OFFICERS, COUNSELLORS AND BUSINESS AGENTS

THE INDEPENDENT UNION OF MASTER CRAFTSMEN
(1934 ———)

NUNN-BUSH SHOP UNION (1932–1934)

NUNN-BUSH COOPERATIVE ASSOCIATION (1915–1932)

OFFICERS

Emmett Dwyer, President 1934
Harry M. Bart, President 1935–1939
Joseph F. Bunk, President 1940–1947
Walter R. Wrasse, President 1948
Walter Romans, President 1949–1950
Esther Ristau, Financial Sec'y & Treas. ...... 1927———

BUSINESS AGENTS

Arthur Becker .. 1923–1928 .. 1932–1935 .. 1943–1946 .. 1949–1950
Arthur Hamilton 1915–1918
Louis Karl 1919–1920
Otto Kahn 1921–1922
Emmett Dwyer 1929–1931
Walter Shenk 1936–1940
Harry Bart 1941
Edward Schneck 1942
Edgar Hilty 1947–1948

RECORDING SECRETARIES AND COUNSELLORS

John L. Waddleton 1934–1941
Louis C. Ritter .... 1942———

Appendix D

SAMPLE LABOR CONTRACT

The following sample contract is largely a duplicate of the one under which the Nunn-Bush Shoe Company and the Industrial Union of Master Craftsmen operated at the time I left the Company on October 31, 1950. It does, however, embrace some of the changes made in later contracts and excludes some material only applicable to this particular business.

AGREEMENT
by and between
_____ Company and _____ Union

THIS AGREEMENT, made this ___ day of _____, _____, by and between the _____ Company (hereinafter called the "MANAGEMENT"), by its duly authorized representative or agent, and the _____ Union (hereinafter called the "UNION"), by its duly authorized representatives or agents.

WHEREAS, the management and the union have heretofore for a considerable number of years engaged in the development and promulgation of a cooperative and friendly association, inuring to the mutual benefit and success of both parties, and

WHEREAS, the management and the union are desirous of a permanent continuance of this harmonious relationship, not only with respect to employment and such matters as remuneration, hours of labor, strikes, layoffs, etc., but also with respect to the production and manufacture of _____ and the sales and earnings, for capital, labor, and management

NOW THEREFORE, in consideration of their mutual promises, the parties hereto agree as follows:

PART 1

Exclusive Negotiating Rights

The management agrees that for the period of this contract it will and it does hereby recognize the union as the exclusive negotiating agent for all workers employed by the ——————— Company who are not direct agents of management.

The management agrees and acknowledges that the jurisdiction of the union includes all production workers and all other factory workers in the plant of the ——————— Company, and those workers employed in the shipping department and office, as well as maintenance workers and other workers, including machinists, housekeepers, porters, etc., but not including executives, semi-executives, foremen, and assistant foremen, who are designated the direct agents of management.

PART II

Factory and Shipping Department

Except as otherwise indicated, the following terms under Part II of this contract shall be applicable only to factory and shipping department workers.

Reward of Labor

Definition, Gross Amount, Determination

The parties hereto agree that capital, management, and labor are each necessary to one another for the success of the business of the ——————— Company, and that therefore they are partners in production insofar as reaping the benefits and fruits of their respective endeavors.

The parties further agree that _____ percent of the wholesale added value of the product produced during this agreement shall be a fair reward for labor's interest.

The percentage as hereinbefore set forth shall be computed on the basis of an average for the twelve preceding months, in which said percentage shall be the percentage of said raw materials as described in schedule "A" hereto attached and made a part of this agreement.

In determining the wholesale value of the product during the term of this agreement, the prevailing wholesale price at the time of completion shall be used, except that allowance shall be made for damaged product and said allowance shall be determined in the manner established by usual custom.

Allowance for the cost of New Employees

When unusual and extraordinary conditions prevail in the labor market, the SHARE-PRODUCTION FUND as heretofore referred to shall be credited for the loss occurring in wages paid to new employees who terminate their employment within sixty-five days of commencing employment.

Changes in the Wholesale Price-List of Product

The management further agrees to consult the executive board of the union upon any contemplated changes in the wholesale price of product before instituting the same, and such procedure shall be a condition precedent with a change in said price. And the management further agrees that it will endeavor to reflect the prevailing market cost in the pricing of its product.

Changes in Economic Conditions

Both parties recognize that there may be changes in the economic conditions or some other circumstances presently not within the knowledge of the said parties and which changes and/or circumstances may cause a change in the fair ratio of the amounts paid to capital, management, and labor interests of the ——————— Company. And consequently either party may upon ten (10) days notice to the other request a reconsideration of the amounts paid to their respective interests. Any adjustment made in such amounts shall be retroactive to the commencement of the quarter in which the said notice was given.

Statement of Associates' Status in the Fund

The management further agrees to give free access to the necessary books of the company and full cooperation to any fully accredited and certified public accountant or accountants selected by the said union to check the added value of the product manufactured during the life of this agreement and the earnings paid out to the workers' Share-Production Fund. The management further agrees to forward to the union each month during the term of this agreement its most accurate estimate of the status of the workers' Share-Production Fund, individually and collectively.

Payment of Earnings above Drawings

When the earnings of the share-production workers employed in the factory and shipping departments exceed the drawings, the same shall be paid to them on or before the fifteenth day of the second month following the accrual thereof, unless some other date for such payment shall be approved by the executive board of the union and management.

Drawing Account

Share-Production Workers

In order to effect an orderly distribution of the union members' share of the company's production, the parties hereto agree that a drawing account system for associates, as hereinafter more fully set forth, shall be employed. The percentage of the added value of the company's product shall constitute the "labor interest" as hereinabove referred to.

Interest on Reserve Account

Management further agrees to pay interest on the balance of the individual reserve accounts of the share-production workers at the prevailing rate of yield of government securities in which such balance is invested; except, however, such computation shall be made at the end of the month in accordance with the adjustments made in the individual account of each member.

Differential and Drawing Rates

It is agreed that, during the period of this agreement, changes may be made in the differential rates upon mutual agreement by and between the executive board of the union and the management.

It is agreed for the purpose of calculating the drawing account of each individual share-production worker, a yearly differential rate of two thousand and eighty (2,080) or 40 X 52, multiplied by the present average hourly drawing, shall be the basis of calculation. However, adjustments in individual rates may be made during the period of this agreement, but such individual adjustment shall not be effective or paid until approved by the executive board of the union; provided, however, that when production department workers are called to do maintenance work, they shall receive compensation at a rate agreed upon by and between the management and the executive board of the union; provided, further, that the differential rates of the president of the union and members of the executive board shall not be reduced during the term of office because of the time spent in the discharge of union business.

Classification of Membership

The labor interest of factory and shipping department workers shall consist of the following classifications of the membership, and the rights, interest, and benefits of each classification, to wit:

The class "A" membership of factory workers shall consist of those workers whose service record began with the _____ Company prior to March 1, 1942, and such workers who have attained a class "A" rating since said time, except those workers who, because of disqualification as hereinafter more fully set forth, were unable to attain the class "A" membership. The class "A" membership of shipping department workers shall consist of those workers employed in the shipping department of the _____ Company who have attained the rating prior to the signing and ensealing of this agreement. The class "A" membership shall constitute a permanent labor force and shall not be subject to layoff. The class "A" workers are to share exclusively in whatever production can be secured by the management until such time as increased production necessitates additional workers as hereinafter enumerated.

The total membership of the class "A" workers employed in the factory is limited to _____ and the total membership of the class "A" workers employed in the shipping department is limited to _____; and the said membership of factory and shipping department workers shall include those class "A" members or workers who attain a class "A" membership while on leave of absence are preserved when promotions to class "A" membership are made.

The class "B" members shall consist of those workers, except those as hereinafter or hereinbefore classified as otherwise, who have been employed in the factory or the shipping department of the _____ Company for a period of at least two (2) years. These class "B" members shall immediately begin to participate in the Share-Production Plan, at the commencement of the first month after the second anniversary of their employment; and class "B" members shall be entitled to all the rights and benefits of the class "A" membership, except that they are subject to layoff in accordance with this agreement.

The class "C" membership shall consist of all workers who had not reached the age of forty-five (45) years at the time of their commencement of employment, such members, of course, being members in good standing in the Industrial Union of Master Craftsmen, but who shall have served less than two (2) years.

The class "D" membership shall consist of those workers who are forty-five years of age or more at the commencement of their employment with the company and who have not previously earned a higher classification as hereinbefore set forth.

The class "DB" membership shall consist of those class "D" members who have completed at least two (2) years of employment with the company. However, such class "DB" members shall at no time be eligible for promotion to class "A" or "B".

The class "HA" membership shall consist of those workers who were previously classified as class "A" members but who, because of their physical or mental impediment, were unable to perform the minimum work provided in the various factory and shipping department schedules and consequently were taken out of the Share-Production Plan upon agreement by and between the executive board of the union and management. Such members are to be paid wages on an hourly basis; otherwise they shall have the same rights and benefits of the class "A" membership with respect to layoffs.

The class "HB" membership shall consist of those workers who were previously classified as class "B" members but who, on account of some physical or mental impediment, could not perform the minimum amount of work provided in the various factory and shipping department schedules and consequently were taken out of the Share-Production Plan. Such members shall be paid wages on an hourly basis.

The class "B" members shall be promoted to the class "A" membership according to seniority upon vacancy occurring in the class "A" membership hereinbefore set forth and agreed upon as being limited to _____ class "A" members in the factory and _____ class "A" members in the shipping department, due to death, resignation, discharge, and/or permanent termination of employment.

All class "A," "B," and "DB" members are to share equally in production in accordance with the present existing agreement with management.

All class "A," "B," "C," "D," "DB," and "HB" members may be laid off when production needs are not sufficient to maintain class "A" members working at least forty (40) hours per week. In the event of necessity of layoff, there shall be no discrimination between "C" and "D" members, except on the basis of seniority rights. In the event of further layoff, there shall be no discrimination between classes "B" and "DB" members except on the basis of seniority rights.

In the event there should be any unusual circumstances or extraordinary contingency arise in the maintenance of production schedule, an exception may be made to the terms of this agreement relating to "layoffs" and the respective rights of all classes of membership, which said exception shall be only on agreement by and between the executive board of the union and the management.

Classes "HA," "HB," "C," and "D" members are wage-earners only and work for a stipulated amount per hour; the total of their wages being paid out of the gross share of the Share-Production Fund before any balance is allocated to the accounts of classes "A," "B," and "DB."

The earnings of classes "A," "B," and "DB" members are to be allocated to the individual account of each member, that member being paid in cash any balance to his or her credit after providing for a reserve fund of twenty-five (25) percent of his or her estimated annual income, or such other reserve fund as agreed upon by and between the executive board of the union and management; the reserve includes provision for sick leave as hereinafter more fully set forth. However, the amount of the reserve fund may be decreased or increased by agreement between the executive board of the union and management.

Stabilized Annual Income

Drawing for Each Week

For the purpose of stabilizing the annual earnings of the workers of the company within the union's jurisdiction, it is agreed by said parties that it will be the joint effort and endeavor on their part to see that each share-production worker shall receive at least one (1) drawing for each week except in such cases of leave of absence or layoff by reason of penalty, and that amount of such drawing will be at least one fifty-second (1/52) of the member's yearly differential rate, except as that differential rate may be changed in accordance with the provisions permitting adjustment of the individual rate and except as the multiplier can be changed in accordance with the provisions hereinafter relating to "overdraft."

Adjustments in Individual Accounts

The adjustment in individual accounts shall be made at the end of each month, and when the reserve in any individual account exceeds twenty-five (25) percent of the annual differential rate, or any other amount in the reserve found as agreed upon by and between the executive board of the union and management, the excess shall be paid on or before the fifteenth day of the second month following its accrual; permission being granted to management to include said excess in the regular weekly drawing, provided, however, that in increasing the amount of the reserve fund, upon agreement between the executive board of the union and management, the amount to be paid in excess of twenty-five percent (25%), until the agreed reserve shall be reached, shall be determined by the executive board of the union. Furthermore, the executive board shall have the right upon agreement by management to extend the payment of the excess earnings on the fifteenth day of the second month following its accrual for certain unusual and extraordinary circumstances.

However, in order that the classes "A," "B," and "DB" members employed in the factory and shipping department may have more uniform and regular drawings of earnings which exceed the amount required for reserve fund, the following plan is hereby adopted, namely: the cost of raw materials shall be determined by applying the monthly inventories to the books of the company. These raw materials for the twelve (12) months from _____ through _____ are totaled and applied to the value of production for this same period and an average percentage of cost of raw materials obtained. This percentage then determines the percentage balance of the added value. Upon completion of the full twelve (12) month cycle from _____ to _____; the average of each succeeding month is computed by dropping the oldest month, when the latest month is added; at all times using the twelve (12) months of operation for which the figures are available in averaging the "added value" for the credits to be made during the current month.

Reserve and Overdraft

The parties agree that it is highly advisable to establish a reserve in the worker's fund of each individual class "A," "B," and "DB" member, in order to guard against the disruption of drawing schedules due to adverse business conditions; and both parties agree to promote the accumulation and maintenance of such reserve. Commencing _____, this reserve shall consist of twenty-five percent (25 %) of the annual differential rate, the same being computed by multiplying the present hourly average drawing by 2,080; however, such reserve may be increased or decreased upon agreement by and between the executive board of the union and management. The said twenty-five percent (25 %) individual reserve account or such other reserve account as shall be agreed upon by and between the executive board of the union and management shall also include drawings for sick leave or other purposes as agreed upon by and between the executive board and management. However, management shall continue to pay the regular weekly drawing, including weeks with holidays and vacation, if by so doing the individual reserve is not reduced below five percent (5 %) of the annual differential rate; but no monthly or adjusted compensation payment will be made if by so doing the reserve is reduced to a sum less than twenty-five percent (25 %) of the annual differential rate or such other amount as agreed upon by and between the executive board of the union and management; provided that if an individual class "A," "B," or "DB" member should require additional drawings from said reserve by reason of his or her absence from his or her daily employment, due to illness, pregnancy, or other emergency, it may be paid as agreed upon by and between the executive board of the union and management; and provided further, that no approval shall be necessary for the drawing of the equivalent of forty (40) hours per week because of illness but that the same shall be paid upon certification of the executive board member of his or her department, the business agent, and management; and provided further, that in no event shall the reserve account of any member be less than five percent (5 %) of his or her annual differential rate; and provided further, such drawing from the reserve for the purposes herein stated shall be at the regular drawing rate. Further, workers who are entitled to draw from their reserves shall not be permitted to draw more than forty (40) hours during any work week; moreover, workers who draw because of the factory closing, due to excessive heat or other contingencies, shall not draw more than for forty hours.

When it is apparent that because of adverse business conditions or downward drift in prices the reserve account may be depleted if no change is made, the drawing account rate shall be revised by agreement between the executive board of the union and management to a point where the reserve at no time will be less than five percent (5%) of the annual differential rate, except as hereinafter stated.

Minimum Wage and Drawing Rates

The minimum wages and differential rates to be paid to associates and "employees" shall be an amount set by law and agreed upon between management and the executive board of the union.

The rates of the various operations in the factory and shipping department and/or of the individual worker shall be fixed according to agreement between the executive board of the union and management, it being understood that a standard base-rate compensation for the various operations in the shipping department will be fixed, the same as operations in the factory considered to be similar in value.

Government Regulations

In establishing a minimum payment of wages and annual differential rates, the present minimum wage-and-hour law was taken as the basis, and therefore the provisions of this contract shall be subject to change in the event the government shall by due enactment increase the minimum wage. Also, members recognized as substandard by the Fair Labor Standards Act Authorities or by the National Labor Relations Act may be paid at the rate approved by said authorities.

Privilege of Being an Associate

It is agreed between the parties hereto that all workers employed at an hourly wage shall be designated "employees."

After a factory or shipping department worker has served a period of two years and shall be eligible for admission to class "A," "B," or "DB," in accordance with the foregoing, he or she shall be given the privilege of associating himself or herself with the share-production workers, and upon his or her acceptance shall be designated as an "associate."

Hours of Labor and Overtime

The regular hours of labor in the factory and shipping department are eight (8) hours in any one (1) day or forty (40) hours in any one (1) work week, except in vacation and hereinafter named holidays, and the management agrees to exert every effort to prevent the hours falling below forty (40) hours per week.

All class "C," "D," "HA," and "HB" members shall be paid time and one-half (1 1/2) for all time worked in excess of eight (8) hours in any one (1) day and for the ninth hour worked in any one (1) day and for work performed on Saturdays and the following enumerated holidays, and double time for all time worked on Sundays.

All share-production workers shall be paid a premium out of capital's share computed at one-half (1/2) the average hourly earnings for all time worked in excess of eight (8) hours in any one (1) day and for the ninth hour worked in any one (1) day and for work performed on Saturdays and any of the following enumerated holidays and double the average hourly earnings for all time worked on Sundays; the same to be an additional payment, over the regular payment agreed upon in the sharing of production, which shall be designated "overtime."

The holidays are as follows: New Year's Day, Fourth of July, Thanksgiving Day, Christmas Day, Labor Day, and Memorial Day.

Temporary Employees

Temporary employees who are employed on a part-time basis shall receive the same rate of compensation as hereinbefore set forth. Management agrees that it shall absorb and not charge the share-production fund that part of overtime in excess of the rate paid for the regular hours of work, in compliance with the aforegoing provisions of this Section of the contract.

Time Lost

In the event that it shall be necessary to close or shut down the factory of _____ or any department or departments thereof by reason of lack of work, heat, or any other contingencies not within the control of the parties hereto, the share-production workers shall be permitted to draw from their respective reserves the equivalent of the number of hours lost because of the closing of said factory or any department or departments thereof, as agreed upon by and between the executive board of the union and management, it being understood that due to the nature of the work in the shipping department in directly servicing the needs of the customers of the _____ Company, any time lost by virtue of lack of work, heat, or other contingency not within the control of the parties hereto and affecting the operations of the factory will not apply to the workers in the shipping department. However, due consideration will be given to the latter in such event.

Employment

New Employees

The employment of new workers shall be in the control of management, subject to the right of the executive board of the union to approve or reject the employment of such new worker.

Where practical, among the candidates for employment, preference shall be given to dependent members of the present workers' immediate families.

Unless an employee within the jurisdiction of the said union shall make application for membership in the union within thirty (30) days after commencing work at _____ Company, he or she shall be discharged. However, nothing herein stated shall deny the right of the said union to approve or reject the application for membership in the union by such employee or defer the same for cause. And furthermore, any worker under the jurisdiction of the union whom the said union shall have found to be undesirable, shall be discharged upon agreement by and between the executive board of the union and management.

No employee or member of the union shall be discharged without the approval of the executive board of the union. In case of failure in agreement between the union and management, individual cases shall be submitted to arbitration as hereinafter provided, and both parties agree to submit to such arbitration before any other action shall be taken.

New Operations

The management and the union further agree that the adding of a new operation or operations and discontinuance of an old operation or operations will be upon mutual agreement between the executive board of the union and management.

Seniority Rights

The management agrees that, in case of layoffs or promotions, except in the case of promotion of members of the union to supervisory or executive positions, or to semi-executive positions, such as assistant special trust, the following principles of seniority shall apply:

Service Record Defined

The service record of a member of the union shall exist from the date of his or her employment and shall continue until such time as he or she is discharged in accordance with the provisions of this contract, or leave the employment of the company without obtaining a leave of absence. However, any employee hired after the signing of this agreement, having less than six (6) months' service record at the time of his or her layoff shall, upon being rehired, be given credit for only the time actually worked previous to the layoff.

Promotion

Only associates and employees of the company shall be chosen to such positions as assistant foreman, floor-ladies, inspectors, and other positions of like nature.

In promotion within a department, the worker with the longest service record in the department where the opening exists shall be offered the advancement, due consideration being given to the prospect's qualifications and merits.

Management agrees to do all in its power to transfer workers to other departments where there may be an opportunity for advancement, and a worker with one (1) year's service record in a department where no advancement is likely and who has the necessary qualifications, shall have the privilege of transfer to an opening in another department before a new employee is engaged for such a position through the regular channels. It is understood that the service record on the new operation of the member so transferred shall start from the date of transfer and shall not include the time credited in the department from which he or she is transferred.

In the event of a promotion from one operation to another or from one department to another, such worker who is so promoted from one operation to another or from one department to another department shall retain the regular rate of the operation from which he or she has been transferred, but no increase in the rate shall be given to him or her until he or she shall have made up all lost production.

If a worker is promoted to a supervisory position of the ———— Company, such worker shall retain his or her seniority record on the job from which he or she was promoted and shall be entitled to said job he or she vacated when accepting the new assignment.

The management further agrees that encouragement and opportunity shall be given to all members of the union to learn other than their own operation in the ————— manufacturing process.

Management agrees that consideration will be given to any member who, because of advanced years, physical handicap, and/or other impediment, is not capable of maintaining the established rate of production on his or her operation, by transferring that member so incapacitated to an operation in his or her own department suited to his or her ability. It is understood, however, that such transfer shall not affect his or her seniority standing or possibility for promotion of any other member, but the parties agree, however, that these operations chosen by and between the management and the executive board of the union may be set aside from the seniority and reserved for members of the union who are unable, because of advanced years, physical handicap, and/or other impediment, to maintain the standard of production at their own operation. Certain other operations may be set aside in the factory upon agreement by and between the executive board of the union and management for the members who because of advanced years, physical handicap, or other impediment are not capable of maintaining the established rate of production on an operation, and the transfer of such member to such operations shall be on the same basis as the transfer of such members within a department.

In the event of promotion from those departments where advancement is unlikely, the member with the longest service record in the department shall be given the first opportunity, consideration being given, however, to the prospect's qualifications and merits. In the case of promotion, the foreman or department head shall send the transfer slip through both the company's payroll office and the union office, and such transfer shall take effect from the date of the promoted member's learning the operation. Thereafter, if the member does work on any other operation for a day or so or any specified time, it shall not prejudice his or her rights to the job to which he or she was promoted.

Layoffs

No class "A" member of the union may be laid off while other class "A" members are working, except as a disciplinary measure as agreed upon by the management and the executive board of the union. As hereinafter set forth, all class "B," "DB," "C," and "D" members may be laid off in accordance with their seniority record on their respective operation or job, as agreed upon by the executive board of the union and management. As heretofore indicated, the class "A" members shall constitute a permanent labor force and will not be subject to layoffs. Furthermore, no class "A" member shall be required to work less than forty (40) hours per week while there are class "B" and "DB" members working.

Nothing in this section of the contract shall, however, apply to those very unusual circumstances and extraordinary contingencies where a layoff may be necessary regardless of class for a short time, and the layoffs of such members for the specified time shall be only upon agreement by and between the executive board of the union and management.

The major operator may displace in time of layoff a semi-major, minor, or unskilled operator of shorter service record in the same department on any operation at which he or she has worked. Seniority rights shall apply only on the job, except a class "DB" member who was hired as an experienced worker on a temporary basis shall be given an opportunity, in the event of a demotion or layoff, to accept a minor and unskilled operation in accordance with his or her service record.

In rehiring, no member shall be engaged until reasonable effort has been made to rehire all other members laid off subsequent to the said member and who possess a longer service record in the factory or shipping department. No new employee shall be engaged until all members of the union who had been laid off, regardless of the department, shall have been given an opportunity to such open position, and an acceptance of the new operation, regardless of department, by such member of the union who had been laid off will not affect his or her seniority rights in the department from which he or she was laid off.

No new employee shall be engaged until reasonable effort has been made to rehire all other members of the union who had been laid off for reasons other than a penalty and in accordance with the aforegoing.

Leave of Absence

The parties hereto agree that any member granted a leave of absence by and with the approval of the executive board of the union and management shall not forfeit his or her service record during the time of such leave of absence. But such member on leave of absence shall be given notice by mail by management as to the expiration of his or her leave of absence, and such notice shall be forwarded to him or her at least seven (7) days prior to the termination of the said leave of absence. However, nothing stated herein shall deny the right of the union to terminate the employment of the said member if he or she has failed to return to work or obtain an extension of the said leave of absence.

When an employee or member on leave of absence because of illness or disability informs management of his or her return to health, management shall restore such member or employee to the job left by him or her upon the taking of the leave of absence. Management has not this obligation toward members who shall obtain a leave of absence by any other reason than illness or disability (pregnancy being agreed upon as not being considered an illness or disability). Management shall reemploy such other members at the first opportunity; provided, however, that management shall make a job available to those members of the union who are on leave of absence because of their service in the armed forces of the United States or its auxiliaries in accordance with the Universal Military Training & Service Act and the modifications and amendments supplemental and amendatory thereto. Any members on leave of absence, upon reemployment, shall return to their respective classification which they possessed at the time of taking their leave of absence.

PART III
General Terms and Provisions

The following terms and conditions under this section of the contract, designated as Part III, shall apply to all workers under the jurisdiction of the union, including the factory, office, and shipping department.

Termination of Employment

A member of the union shall give at least three (3) days' notice to management before terminating his or her employment. Failure to give the required notice shall subject such member to penalty as imposed upon him or her by the executive board of the union.

Management further agrees that no member of the said union or employee of the _____ Company, shall be discharged for cause and/or reason whatsoever except upon agreement by and between management and the executive board of the union. Employees shall be given _____ days and associates _____ days notice.

Working Conditions and Efficiency

The management and the union further recognize their respective duties and obligations always to strive to cooperate in endeavoring to maintain the highest possible degree of efficiency in the operation of its plant.

The members of the union and the management agree to cooperate in all safety and sanitary regulations pertaining to the _____ Company and its equipment, and said members of the union shall endeavor to assist management in meeting the requirements of the Wisconsin Code for Industrial Safety.

The business agent of the union will express ideas of the members to management with respect to working conditions and safe practices as well as the efficient operation of the factory, office, and shipping department, and said business agent will communicate directly to management on all matters which he deems it necessary to have considered.

Check-Off System

Management agrees to deduct from the weekly drawing or paycheck of each member of the union the dues owing to said union and turn the same over to the financial secretary and treasurer of the union as so deducted.

And management further agrees to deduct from the weekly drawing or paycheck of each new member of the union the initiation fees due to the said union and turn over the amount so deducted to the financial secretary and treasurer of the union.

Administration of Agreement

Management agrees that the principal officers (president, vice-president, recording secretary and counsel, financial secretary, and business agent of the union) shall have free access to the workers in all departments of the _____ Company and shall be free to communicate with other officers of the union and members thereof whenever he, she, or they deem it fit, without let or hindrance of the management and its agents. Management further agrees that the executive board members of the union shall have free access to all workers in the department which they represent without let or hindrance from management or its agents.

Management agrees to recognize the business agent of the union as the personal representative of the union members and employees in the production, office, and shipping departments and to deal with him or her in all matters pertaining to the individual members or to their collective welfare.

The president, business agent, and all other officers of the union heretofore enumerated are to use discretion in the exercise of their powers as to the necessities of management and proper maintenance of discipline and continuous production.

Whenever the business agent is unable to effect the solution of any matter between management and the union, or between management and a member of the union, management agrees to meet with the executive board of the union to consider such matter and proper solution thereof.

The parties agree that when the agents of management and the executive board of the union are unable to satisfactorily adjust any grievance, the same shall be referred forthwith for arbitration to such persons or persons whom the union and management might agree upon.

Both parties agree that the above routine of arbitration shall be a condition precedent to any litigation of their rights and interest under this agreement.

Strike Clause

The parties hereto agree that while this agreement is effective and while a proper solution of any questions arising under this agreement may be had, no lockout, strike, sitdown, boycott, or other stoppage or interference with the work of the management and of the union shall be called, permitted, or maintained.

Capital, Management, and Labor a Partnership

The parties hereto agree that capital, management, and labor are each necessary to one another for the success of the business of the _____Company, and that, therefore, they are partners in a sense of the word, insofar as reaping the benefits and fruits of their respective endeavors is concerned.

Duration of this Agreement

This agreement shall be effective from _____ to _____ inclusive, and thereafter from year to year, unless before _____ _____or the last day of any renewed term, one party gives notice to the other, in writing, that it does not desire to renew this agreement or that it purposes certain changes therein; except that either party may give notice to the other, in writing, in a change of the amount to be allocated to the share-production fund, in accordance with the provisions of the paragraph relating to "Reward of Labor" as hereinbefore set forth.

In witness whereof, the parties hereto have hereunto set their hands and seals this ———————————————

Signed and Sealed in ————————————————

Presence of:

By_____ (SEAL)
President

————————————— ————————————— UNION

————————————— By_____ (SEAL)
President

By_____ (SEAL)

BIBLIOGRAPHY

1. ARGYRIS, CHRIS., *Personality and Organization*, Harper & Bros., 1937.
2. BRANDEIS, LOUIS D., *Business a Profession*, Hale, Cushman & Flint, 1933.
3. CHASE, STUART, *Roads to Agreement*, Harper & Bros., 1951.
4. CHERNICK, JACK, and GEORGE C. HELLICKSON, *Guaranteed Annual Wages*, The University of Minnesota Press, 1945.
5. COMMONS, JOHN R., *Industrial Goodwill*, McGraw-Hill, 1919.
6. DRUCKER, PETER F. *The New Society*, Harper & Bros., 1949.
7. GARDNER, BURLEIGH B., and DAVID G. MOORE, *Human Relations in Industry*, Richard D. Irwin Inc., 1955.
8. GOLDEN, CLINTON S., and HAROLD J. RUTTENBERG, *The Dynamics of Industrial Democracy*, Harper & Bros., 1942.
9. GORDON, THOMAS, *Group Centered Leadership*, Houghton Mifflin, 1955.
10. GOYDER, GEORGE, *The Future of Private Enterprise*, Basil Blackwell, 1954.
11. JAQUES, ELLIOTT, *The Changing Culture of a Factory*, Tavistock Publications, 1951.
12. KING, WILLFORD I., *The Keys to Prosperity*, Constitution and Free Enterprise Foundation, 1948.
13. LEITCH, JOHN, *Man-to-Man*, H. C. Osborn, 1919.
14. LESIEUR, FREDERICK G., *The Scanlon Plan*, John Wiley & Sons, 1958.
15. LINCOLN, JAMES F., *Incentive Management*, The Lincoln Electric Co., 1951.

16. MAIER, NORMAN R. F, *Principles of Human Relations*, John Wiley & Sons, 1952.

17. RUCKER, ALLEN W., *Labor's Road to Plenty*, L. C. Page & Co., 1937.

18. SOMERVELL, HUBERT A., *Industrial Peace in Our Time*, George Allen & Unwin Ltd., 1950.

19. TAWNEY, R. H., *Religion and the Rise of Capitalism*, John Murray, 1943.

Index

Absences, method of handling, 11
Adamson Company, East Palestine, Ohio, 64–66
Administrative personnel, selection of, 123
Agitators, 113–118
  making friends of, 115
  policy of trying to convert, 116–118
Agreements
  methods of reaching, 86–87
  sample labor contract, 192–209
  signing of, 40
Appreciation, need for, 137
Apprenticeship period, 16, 183
  hourly wage rates paid during, 16
Arbitrary power
  in the open shop, 106–110
  in the union shop, 110–111
  misuse of, 106–107
  relinquished by management and labor, 31, 79–99, 163
Arbitration of disputes, 80, 86
  management and union agree to, 5, 7
  rack problem, 91–93
Associates, Share-Production Plan, 183
  classification of, 16–19, 48
  handicapped, 18
  overtime pay, 20–21
  status as sharers in production, 10, 175
  vacations and holidays, 19–20
  yearly differential rate, 11–12
Associations, trade, 167
Authority, managerial, 132–133

Bart, Harry, 37–38, 41
Bates, Johnny, 121–122
Becker, Arthur, 43
Bibliography, 210–211
Board of directors:
  annual meetings, 141–142
  compensation paid officers of the company, 6
  director from factory and from retail stores, 50–51
  labor representatives on, 5, 159–160
  legal liability of, 141
  prerogatives of arbitrary action taken away from, 88–89
  union representation on, 5–6
  vote on officers' salaries, 52–53
  worker-director, 51–52
Bonuses, 54, 66, 142, 151–153
  consulting with union first, 152–153
Books and records of the company, union has access to, 5
Booms and depressions, eliminating, 181
Boss, attitude of workers toward, 124–125
Bush, A. W., 75, 81–82, 88
Businesses:
  objectives of industrial organizations, 178
  participation by labor in, 163

Capital:
  depends on customer who purchases the product, 7
  limitation on return of, 159
  of small corporations, 140–141

Capital and labor, 140–146
  conflict between labor and, 177
  cooperation between, 181
  democratic principles for, 181–184
  membership in national associations, 182
  mutual interests, 171, 175
  shareholders, 140–146
Capitalism
  defects and remedies for, 23–26, 106
  standard of living and, 175, 176
  struggle between communism and, 102
Capital's share
  overtime paid from, 20–21
  service departments charged to, 22
  vacation and holidays paid from, 19–20
Chernick, Jack, 155, 158
Christmas gifts for employees, 148–149
Classification of workers:
  associates, 16–19, 48
  employees, 56
Co-determination, in West Germany, 159–160
Collective bargaining, 65, 110
Common enterprise, democratic principles for, 181–184
Communications between labor and management, consultative management, 160–161, 163
Communist countries:
  economic development, 162
  state operated industries, 162
Company unions, 160–161
Compensation of labor, 62–70
  based on production figures, 9, 25
  computing labor's share, 8–9
  concept of labor as a commodity to be bought and sold, 104
  differential rates, 11–12, 35
  drawings and reserves, 9–11
  executives, 6, 137
  hourly wage rates, 16–18
    tragedy of, 23–26

  incentive pay, 22, 67, 150
  as a just share of production, 7–26
  labor's right to a living wage, 73–74, 102–105
  overtime, 20–21
  paid by customer who purchases the product, 7
  principles of, 62–63
  regularity of pay, 37, 68
  Rucker Plan, 62–68
  salesmen, 103–104
  Scanlon Plan, 64–68
  seasonal variations, 9
  share-production plan, 7–26 (see also Share-production plan)
  tragedy of the fixed hourly wage, 23–26
  at the turn of the century, 164–165
  uniformity of income, 9, 68
  wages compared to net sales, 32–33
Consultative management, developing potential of the worker, 160–161
Contracts, sample labor, 192–209
Cooperation:
  between labor unions and management, 170–172
  fostered by share-production plan, 31–32
  freedom gained through, 81
  method of asking for, 86–87
  plans promote, 69
  possibilities inherent in, 65–66
Corporations:
  income tax laws, 154
  legal liability, 141
  management of, 142
  objective of, 178
  shareholders and labor, 140–146
Crash of 1929, 27–28
Cutters, special incentives paid to, 22–23

Decision-making, workers participate in, 4, 81–99, 182
Democracy, industrial, 3–7

characteristics of political democracy applied to, 89–90
principles of, 61, 181–184
strikes, arbitrary methods relinquished in favor of, 79–99
worker-participation system, 150
workers obey rules they participate in making, 5, 81–99
Differential rates, 11–12
basis for setting weekly drawings, 12
definition, 35
developing scientific, 46–54
1936–38, 48–49
Discharge of employees, 182
Discipline, workers make decisions concerning, 6
Disputes:
democratic procedures, 93, 98–99
employment of married women, 93–94
settled by judicial processes, 61, 99
settlement of, 86–87
smoking problem, 95–96
Dividends paid to shareholders, 142
Drawings, 183
share-production plan, 9–11, 36
Drew, Tom, 74–75
Dulles, Allen, 178

Earnings, based on yearly differential rate, 11–12
Eby, Kermit, 171
Economic Cooperation Administration, 112
Economic efficiency, relationship between psychological values and, 105–106, 118
Economic implications of the plan, 45
Economic laws, relationship between wages and net sales, 32–33
Economy, flexibility in, 163
Eddy-Ricker-Nickels Company, 62
Employment policies (see also Workers)
associates, 16–19

changes in worker attitude, 41–42
classification of employees, 16–20, 56
employees over 45, 16, 18–19
executives, 137–138
job-security provisions, 16–19
new employees selected by management, 15–16
restrictive practices, 111–113
right to secure, in competitive organizations, 129
right to seek employment, 113
30-day probationary period, 15–16
two-year apprenticeship, 16
unfair practices, 112–113
union membership, 15–16
vacations and holidays, 19–20
Employers, at the turn of the century, 165
Enterprise system, democratic principles for, 181–184
Enthusiasm of workers, plan stimulated, 41
Ethics:
managerial, 111–113, 131
value of business standards, 162
Executives (see also Management)
as direct agents of management, 5
employment opportunites, 137–138
health of, 136
power, 181
relations with unions, 170
struggle for advancement, 138–139
subordination of home life to job, 138

Fair Labor Standard Act, 18
52-Paychecks-a-Year Plan, 4, 41, 63
adjusted compensation, 48–49
economic objectives, 63–64
multiplier increases from 37 to 40, 48
Flexibility of share-production plan, 41, 163
Ford, Henry, 179

Foremen:
  authority of, 78–79, 106–110
  as direct agents of management, 5
  misuse of authority, 106–110
  responsibility of, 75
  union must approve appointment
    of, 96–98
Freedom of speech:
  agitators and, 113–118
  workers need, 129
Free-enterprise system:
  advancement in, 103
  dangers to, 177
  defects and remedies for, 23–26
  overcoming trade cycles, 23–26

Genesco, 3
Gifts to employees, 148–149
Glacier Metal Company, London,
    England, 159, 163
Golden, Clinton S., 64
Grievance procedures, 85–86, 94
Guaranteed annual wage plans, 41
  Hormel Plan, 157–159
  Procter & Gamble Plan, 154–156

Hamilton, Arthur, 117–119
Handicapped associates, 18
  paid hourly wages, 18
Harsch, 74, 79, 125–126, 148–149
Hellickson, George C., 155, 158
Holidays and vacations, compensa-
    tion for, 19–20, 39, 110
Hormel, Jay, 157–158
Hormel Plan, 157–159
Hourly wages:
  employees receiving, 16–17
  handicapped associates, 18
  tragedy of the fixed, 23–26

Incentive pay, 22, 67, 150
Income:
  families in U.S., 102
  regularity of, 64
  uniformity of, 9
Income tax laws, effect on profit-
    sharing plans, 154
Independent Union of Master
    Craftsmen, 4–5, 191

Industrial Peace in Our Time (Som-
    ervell), 25
Industrial relations, concept of de-
    mocracy in, 4–7
International Shoe Company, 3

Job security, 64
  provisions affecting, 16–19
Joint council, 31, 86, 94n, 181
  composition of, 31
  opposition to the plan, 36–37
  share-production plan presented
    to, 33–34
Judicial processes, for settling dif-
    ferences, 61, 99

Karl, Louis, 101, 146
Kedian, M. V., 75
King, Mackenzie, 140
Kreckle, Gus, 51–53
Kuecker, Theodore, 51

Labor:
  capital and, 175, 177
  as a commodity to be bought and
    sold, 104, 105
  compensation, 62–70
  computing labor's share, 8–9
  concept of partners in production,
    104
  cost of, 67, 176–177
  exploitation of, 74
  income of, 176
  organization of, 4, 110, 181–182
    (see also Unions)
  overcoming suspicions of, 180–
    181
  relationship between prices and
    the cost of, 67
  sample contract, 192–209
  settlement of disputes, 85–99
  welfare of, 73–74
  workers participate in decisions
    affecting, 73–99
  World War II shortage, 21
Labor-management relations, 73–99
  arbitrary methods relinquished
    by, 79–99

based on mutual trust, 6, 52
democratic principles of, 98–99
disputes settled by judicial processes, 61, 99
flexibility to keep economy in balance, 41, 163
managerial ethics, 111–113
need for cooperative effort, 61
partners in production, 3–26, 150
problems more psychological and economic, 92
reconsideration of compensation, 8–9
Share-Production Plan, 150
yearly differential rates set by, 11–12
Labor's share:
based on total sales, 58, 66
based on value added to raw material, 58–59, 66
Lapointe Machine Tool Company, Hudson, Mass., 65
Lay-off policy, 34–37
Leatherworker's Union, 168–169
LeRoach, Jack, 96–98
Lincoln, Abraham, 173
Lincoln Electric Company, Cleveland, Ohio, 159
Loppnow, Billy, 47–48
Loyalty to company, 184
hourly wage earner, 30
promoting, 15–16
salaried workers, 30

Management, 130–139
actions to prevent union organization, 167–168
agreements with union, 5
arbitrary totalitarian power, 179
association with workers, 130–132
authoritarianism, 78–79, 106–110, 132, 139
benefits from Share-Production Plan, 50–51
chain of command, 133–134
compensation, 137
democratic leadership, 179–180

difficulty of changing jobs, 137–138
drive for status, 134–135
duties and responsibilities, 6, 98
ethics, 111–113, 131
impressing the man in authority, 134–135
individualist scarce in, 135
lower and middle, 137, 139
managers have to subordinate home life to job, 138
need for recognition and appreciation, 137, 139
new employees selected by, 15
new role of, 173–184
organization charts, 132–133
overcoming labor's suspicions, 180–181
prerogative to fix wage rates, 79
president and vice-presidents, 130–131
rating of ability, 135
relationship of managers to the boss and to each other, 133–134
specialization, 136–137
struggle for advancement, 138–139
surrendered power to make unilateral decisions in 1919, 3
unions and, 132, 182
women's position, 138
worker's confidence in fairness of, 52–53
Materials, incentives for saving, 63
Motivation:
by other than economic factors, 147
by various types of welfare schemes, 148

National Chamber of Commerce, 167, 178
National Labor Relations Act, 18, 53n, 94n, 114, 168
unfair practices, 113, 115
National Manufacturers Association, 167
Nunn, H. L., 38

Nunn-Bush Shoe Company:
  annual business, 3
  computing labor's share, 8–9
  financial crisis after First World
    War, 145–146
  founding of, 3, 75
  number of employees, 3
  reputation and success of, 69–70
  stock purchase plans, 144–145
Nunn-Bush Cooperative Association, 82–85
Nunn-Bush Plan (see Share-Production Plan)
Nunn-Bush Profit-Sharing and Retirement Fund, 187
Nunn-Bush Savings and Profit-
  Sharing Plan, 186

Organization, industrial, 132
Output, restriction of, 123–124
Overtime pay, 20–21, 110, 153

Paternalism and welfare plans, 147–
  163
Pension plans, 183
  provisions of, 184
Piece-work system, 150–151
Pollnow, Ray, 119–120
Praise, importance of, 118–121
President of company:
  association with workers, 130
  duties and responsibilities, 130–
    131
Prices and pricing:
  effect of fixed hourly wages on,
    23–26
  fixed by both management and
    labor, 6
  wholesale prices, 9
  workers interested in, 42–43
Procter & Gamble Plan, 154–156
Production:
  committees, 181
  compensation based on, 9
  effect of fixed hourly wages on,
    23–26
  financial incentives to increase,
    150

workers interested in schedules,
  42
Profit-sharing plans, 153–154
Profits, distribution of excess to
  shareholders and workers,
  146
Promotion policies, 15–16
  based on merit, 123
  principle of seniority, 121–123
  promotion from within, 15
Psychological values:
  importance of recognition, 118–
    121
  principle of seniority, 121–123
  relationship between economic
    efficiency and, 105–106, 118
Publicity, share-production plan,
  41, 64

Racine Radiator Company, 41
Rates and schedules, developing
  scientific, 46–54
Raw materials, labor's share based
  on value added to, 58–59
Recognition, importance of, 118–
  121
  management needs, 137
Redfield, Jim, 109–110
References from former employers,
  111–112
Rejects, reducing number of, 63
Reserves, Share-Production Plan,
  9–11, 183
  decision to set up, 55–56
  invested in Government securi-
    ties, 10
  method of building, 10
Restriction of output, 123–124
Retail Store and Department Divi-
  sion, 51
Retirement plans, 183, 184, 186–
  190
  company's contribution, 187–188
  management's obligations, 189–
    190
Ritter, Louis, 94
Roberts, Johnson & Rand Shoe Co.,
  St. Louis, 73–74
Rucker, Allen W., 58, 59, 62–68

Rucker Share of Production Plan, 63–68
  labor's share based on value added to raw material, 58, 66
Rules and regulations, mutually agreed upon, 182

Sales, wages compared to net, 32–33
Salesmen, compensation of, 103–104
Scanlon, Joseph, 64–68
Scanlon Plan, 64–68, 171
Schenk, Walter, 116–117
Schneck, Ed, 121–122
Schwanburg, Arthur, 49
Scott, Ben, 163
Scott & McHale Shoe Company, Ontario, Canada, 64, 66, 163
Scrimshaw, Stewart, 85, 88
Sears-Roebuck company, 186
Seniority:
  importance to workers, 121–123
  job-security provisions and, 16–19
  for rights and guarantees, 3
Service departments, 21–23
Severance pay, 129
Share-Production Plan, 7–26
  absences from work, 11
  advantages, 173
  associates, 10, 56, 183
    statement of associate's share, 185
  attitude of labor leaders toward, 171
  benefits of, 37
  calculations for a hypothetical pay period, 12–15
  change in worker attitude, 41–42
  changes in, 55
    method of figuring labor's share, 59–61
  classification of employees, 56
  compared with other plans, 66–67

  compensation based on just share of production, 7–26
  conception of, 27–39
    approved by secret ballot, 38–40
    52 payments a year, 34
    labor opposition, 33–34
    opposition by workers, 36–37
    plan approved by union, 37–39
  democracy in industrial relations, 4–7, 181–184
  dictatorship replaced with democratic leadership, 179
  drawings and reserves, 9–11, 36, 55–56
  each worker shares in proportion to his contribution to production, 36
  employment and promotion policies, 15–16
  explaining it to workers, 43–44
  52-Paychecks-a-Year Plan, 41
    (see also 52-Paychecks-a-Year Plan)
  graduated scale of percentages for labor, 57–58
  importance of plan, 173
  job-security provisions, 16–19, 37
  labor agreements and, 7–8, 67
  lay-off policy, 34–36
  not a guaranteed annual wage plan, 41
  overtime, 20–21
  publicity given plan, 41, 64
  reconsideration by labor and management, 8–9
  regularity of pay, 37
  reserves, 9–11, 36, 55–56
  service departments, 21–22
  special provisions, 21–23
  for supervisors, 36
  tragedy of the fixed hourly wage, 23–26
  two-year apprenticeship required, 10
  vacations and holidays, 19–20
  workers become self-respecting, 150
World War II, 56

World War II (*cont.*)
 yearly differential rates, 11–12, 35, 46–54
  basis for setting weekly drawings, 12
Shareholders:
 buy listed stocks, 141
 dividends, 142
 excess profits distributed to, 142–146
 labor and, 140–146
 liability of, 141
 small corporations, 140–141
 workers and junior executives as, 144–145
Sick leave, 110
Small businesses, management and labor, 161–162
Smoking problem, 95–96
Somervell, Hubert, 25
Soviet Russia, production of, 178
Standard of living, 175, 176
Status:
 attitude of worker influenced by changes in, 175
 of managers, 134–135
 women factory workers, 127
Stint system, 151
Stock purchase plans, 144–145
Stocks:
 capital shares sold to workers, 154
 liability of shareholders, 141
 small businesses, 140–141
Strege, Art, 100–101
Strikes:
 losses due to, 77
 Milwaukee shoe factories, 1914, 75–81
 threats of, 78
Supervisors (*see also* Foremen)
 appointment discussed with business agent, 96–98
 relationship between worker and, 124–125
 share-production plan for, 36

Tawney, R. H., 147n
Technological advances, effect on wages, 45–46

Time-study and rate-making, 6, 47–48
Tyler, Gus, 172

Unemployment, alleviating, 181
Unions, 164–172
 agreement to changing method of figuring labor's share, 59–61
 agreements with management, 5
 appointment of supervisors approved by, 96–98
 arbitrary power in union shops, 110–111
 assigned man to work with time-study engineer, 47–48
 business agent, 43, 47, 83, 85, 118
  concerned with production schedules, 48
  power of, 169
 company, 160–161
 constitution and by-laws, 82–83, 88–89
 democratic concept of, 169
 differential rates of officers, 12
 dues, 84–85
  collection of, 182
 duties and responsibilities, 6
 executive board, 44
 grievance procedures, 85–86
 has access to books and records of the company, 5
 health and death benefit plans, 84
 historical development, 164–168
 importance of explaining plan to, 44–45
 Independent Union of Master Craftsmen, Nunn-Bush Co., 4–5, 191
 joint council, 31, 86, 94n, 181
 leaders, 169–170
 membership, 15, 82, 84
 membership on board of directors, 5, 53
 need for cooperation between management and, 170–172
 Nunn-Bush Cooperative Association, 82–85
 open shop, 167
 organizers, 164

Unions (*cont.*)
    paid secretary and lawyer advise
        worker director, 5
    progress made by leaders, 167
    radical, 75
    role of, 164–172
    sample labor contract, 192–209
    shop committee, 53
    30-day probationary period, 84

Vacations and holidays, 110
    compensation for, 19–20
    paid, 39

Waddleton, John, 52
Wages (*see also* Compensation)
    compared to net sales, 32–33
    right of management to fix, 79
    wage-rate fallacy, 62, 67
    workers restricted to a bare "liv-
        ing wage," 102–105
Wagner Act, 53n, 168, 177–178
Weldon, W. E., 75, 88
Welfare plans, 147–163
    bonus schemes, 151–153
    capital shares sold to workers,
        154
    co-determination, 159–160
    consultative management and
        company unions, 160–161
    demeaning nature of, 162–163
    fallacy in use of, 148
    Hormel Plan, 157–159
    limitation of capital's return, 159
    paternalism and, 147–163
    piece-work system, 150–151
    Proctor & Gamble Plan, 154–156
    profit-sharing, 153–154
    stint system, 151
Wilson, Woodrow, 90
Women in industry, 125–128
    importance of status, 127
    opportunities in management,
        138
Work schedules, 6
    developing scientific, 46–54
Workers, 100–129
    advancement opportunities, 103

agitators and freedom of speech,
    113–118
arbitrary power in the open shop,
    106–110
attitude toward boss, 124–125
attitude toward fellow workers,
    48
attitudes affect economic effi-
    ciency, 102
capital shares sold to, 154
distribution of stock to, 146
freedom of speech, 90, 113–118
importance of recognition, 118–
    121
increasing self-respect and dig-
    nity of, 81
insecure position of, 102
managerial ethics, 111–113
morale of, 114
need for satisfaction, 101
participate in making rules, 81–
    99
plan changed attitude of, 41
presenting gifts to, 148–149
purchases of company stock, 144–
    145
restriction of output, 123–124
restriction to a bare "living wage,"
    102–105
right to seek employment, 111–
    113
risk taken by, 142–143
seniority, 121–123
should receive share of excess
    profits, 142–146
social and psychological attitudes,
    105–106
status, 103
women in industry, 125–128
Workers' executive board, 94
Workmanship, incentives for good,
    63, 70
World War II, labor shortage, 21

Young, Fred, 41

Zygalowski, Eddie, 174–175